FIGHTING FORCE

The 90th Anniversary of the Royal Air Force

FIGHTING FORCE

The 90th Anniversary of the Royal Air Force

Photography and text by
JAMIE HUNTER

TOUCHSTONE
BOOKS LTD

First published in 2008 by Touchstone Books Ltd

Copyright © Touchstone Books Ltd 2008

Touchstone Books Ltd, Highlands Lodge, Chartway Street,
Sutton Valence, Kent ME17 3HZ, United Kingdom.

A copy of the CIP data for this book is available from
the British Library upon request.

The rights of Jamie Hunter to be identified as the
author of this work have been asserted in accordance
with Section 77 of the Copyright, Designs and Patents
Act of 1988.

Photography by Jamie Hunter unless otherwise credited
Designed by Sue Pressley and Paul Turner
Edited by Anthony John

Printed and bound in Italy

ISBN: 978-0-9551020-5-9

Fighting Force has been produced with the full
support of the Royal Air Force to give an overview
of today's modern RAF. Author and photographer
Jamie Hunter has been given exclusive access to
the squadrons and personnel of the RAF, in order to
write informative and authoritative text, and to
obtain exciting and previously unpublished imagery
to portray a contemporary air force providing
expeditionary air power in the 21st Century.
www.raf.mod.uk

Page 1: The dynamic world of fast-jet flying – a Panavia Tornado F3 of No 56(R) Squadron streaks skyward.

Page 2: The latest superfighter – a Eurofighter Typhoon F2 of No 29(R) Squadron.

Page 3: The backbone of the RAF strike force – a Panavia Tornado GR4 of No XIII Squadron.

Right: Two C-130Js head out from RAF Lyneham for a training mission. The 'Super' Hercules J-model is operated by Nos 24 and 30 Squadrons.

Pages 6 and 7: Harrier in your face – one of the RAF's most famous aircraft – the BAE Systems Harrier GR9.

Page 8: The Eurofighter Typhoon is a true multi-role fighter bomber with growth potential to meet future demands of the RAF.

CONTENTS

FOREWORD
by HRH The Duke of Edinburgh

BUCKINGHAM PALACE.

Both the Army and the Royal Navy were quick to recognise the potential value of aircraft fairly early. The Royal Flying Corps was established in 1912, and the Royal Naval Air Service two years later. Although both Services maintained a separate aviation capability, experience during the First World War suggested that an independent air service would best meet the demands of the overall strategy for the defeat of the Central Powers. 90 years ago, on 1 April 1918, the RNAS and the RFC were merged to form the Royal Air Force, to become the first independent Air Force anywhere in the world.

In retrospect, it would seem that the aircraft and weapons of those early days were somewhat primitive, but they were the best that the technology of the time could provide. Since those days, the only thing about the RAF that has not changed is the quality of the men and women who served, and are serving, with it. Aircraft, engines and weapons continue to be subject to the development of technology, while operational and domestic management systems are under constant review.

This book celebrates the 90th anniversary of the formation of the RAF and illustrates the way in which it has responded to the demands of the ever-changing international situation. The pioneers were challenged to solve the problems of their day; 90 years later their successors face the same challenges. The demand for commitment, skill and endurance, as well as for imagination, foresight, initiative and judgement, is as great as ever.

Philip

FIGHTING FORCE
The 90th Anniversary of the Royal Air Force

Introduction by Air Chief Marshal Sir Glenn Torpy
KCB CBE DSO ADC BSc(Eng) FRAeS FCGI RAF

Chief of the Air Staff

The Royal Air Force in 2008 traces its history back to 1 April 1918 through the merger of the Royal Flying Corps and the Royal Naval Air Service, both of which were forged in the bitter conflict of World War I. From the very early use of artillery spotting balloons it was clear that air power was likely to have a significant impact on the conduct of future warfare. Technology was at the heart of this early capability, and quickly allowed the first fighter pilots to engage in aerial combat in the skies over the battlefields of Northern France. Now, 90 years on, we have moved from Vickers machine guns to advanced radar-guided air-to-air missiles and precision-guided bombs that are capable of striking a target within a few metres anywhere on the globe. The rich 90-year history of the RAF tracks and charts the major advances and cutting-edge developments in military aviation. From the very start,

the RAF has worked tirelessly to maintain its combat edge, to enhance its reputation for excellence and to develop the incredible 'Fighting Force' that exists today.

The Birth of an Air Force

The RAF was the world's first independent Air Force, born as a direct result of aerial warfare's success in WW1. Major General Hugh Trenchard, the first Chief of Air Staff and the acknowledged 'Father' of the RAF wrote, "the whole Service was practically a war creation on a temporary basis, without any possibility of taking into account that it was going to remain on a permanent basis". Many initially viewed the creation of the RAF as a temporary administrative step, but Trenchard was clear that he was going to create a permanent new force, with what he declared to be 'Air Force spirit'. After an extremely difficult start, during

Above: Thumbs up! An RAF Harrier GR9 pilot ready for action.

Left: Tornado F3 accelerates dramatically.

Opposite: A heavily-laden Eurofighter Typhoon FGR4 of No 17(R) Squadron 'tips in' on its target.

Previous pages: Spitfire MkIIa leads Typhoon F2.

which numerous questions were raised over the need for an independent force, Trenchard skilfully and resolutely guided the RAF through its early years, and in the process laid the foundations for the RAF we know today. From its inception, the RAF has been maintained as a highly efficient and exceptionally well-trained force, ready to adapt to emerging threats and new opportunities. Trenchard saw quality training as a key part of the Service, and the creation of the RAF Colleges at RAF Cranwell and RAF Halton are testaments to this belief.

Supporting the United Kingdom at Home and Abroad

The inter-war years saw the RAF extensively involved in air policing duties in the Middle East and North-West Frontier but its greatest test came with the outbreak of World War II. The Battle of Britain remains to this day the iconic and outstanding feat of aerial warfare, and the determination and bravery of the young fighter pilots who defended the United Kingdom are a

permanent part of the RAF's ethos and heritage. But we must also pay homage to the far greater number of courageous bomber crews that flew repeatedly deep into the heart of Germany; to the airmen who served on Operations in the Far East; and to the thousands of airmen and airwomen back in the United Kingdom who kept the aircraft and crews flying day after day. This rich and varied history underpins the sense of pride and professionalism that pervades the squadrons and units of today's RAF.

Since WW2, air power has played a vital – and in some cases decisive – role in every conflict. Credible, high-readiness Air Forces played a major part in bringing the Cold War to an end but the Falklands War will also always be remembered as an extraordinary feat of military – and aviation – achievement. Although the collapse of the Warsaw Pact resulted in a gradual reduction in the size of all three Services, technology delivered significant increases in capability through the introduction of aircraft like the Tornado. The First Gulf War, Operation Deliberate Force in Bosnia and

Operation Allied Force in Kosovo all demonstrated the ability of air power to shape the battlespace and deliver decisive effect. For the 12 years following the First Gulf War, air power was also used in the Northern and Southern No-Fly Zones of Iraq to contain the Saddam regime in a form that was acceptable to the International Community.

While operations in the Middle East and the Balkans dominated the 1990s, the RAF also took part in numerous peace support, evacuation and humanitarian relief operations. In 1994, following civil war in Rwanda, and in Angola in 1995, the RAF deployed aircraft to support British Army units engaged in UN humanitarian missions. RAF air transport assets also evacuated British nationals from trouble spots such as Ethiopia in June 1998, Sierra Leone in December 1998, Côte d'Ivoire in November 2004, as well as flying mercy missions to areas struck by natural disasters, including the tsunami in South-East Asia and earthquakes in Pakistan. Responsiveness, reach and speed are all key to delivering success in these types of operations, and

the RAF has played a vital role in providing timely medical aid, supplies and support to these devastated parts of the world.

The RAF, along with its fellow Services, has also assisted the civil authorities in the United Kingdom and has regularly provided support and assistance to the civil community. In recent years, extensive support was given to help with the effects of flooding in Central and Southern England and Wales; to support the farming community during foot and mouth epidemics; and to provide essential emergency cover following the Firemen's strike. The RAF is also a major plank in the United Kingdom's Search and Rescue capability, with the yellow Sea King helicopters of the RAF providing critical support to HM Coastguard, the Royal National Lifeboat Institute and Mountain Rescue Teams.

Force Structure

Today, the RAF is as vital to the United Kingdom as it has ever been. Events over the past 25 years demonstrate the unpredictable and volatile nature of the world, and the need for high-readiness forces that have the reach, speed and firepower to deliver immediate effect. This is just what air power provides and, as a result, it remains a key tool for demonstrating political intent, setting the conditions for follow-on forces and contributing to a broader military campaign. History confirms the vital – and sometimes decisive – role that air power plays in every campaign, whether it is

providing strategic and battlefield mobility; intelligence, surveillance and reconnaissance; command and control; force protection; precise and timely fire power; or, most importantly, control of the air. These capabilities are just as important today in the fight against global terrorism.

In order to preserve the robustness and quality of the RAF's expeditionary front-line capability the Service has implemented a range of measures to improve efficiency and effectiveness. On 1 April 2007, Headquarters Personnel and Training Command and Headquarters Strike Command merged to form Headquarters Air Command RAF High Wycombe. Integral to Air Command are Numbers 1, 2 and 22 Groups. No 1 Group is the co-ordinating organisation for all front-line fast-jet elements and consists of some 12,000 personnel. The Group is responsible for the air defence of the United Kingdom, using the Eurofighter Typhoon F2, Tornado F3 and ground and airborne radar systems, and also supports operations in Iraq and Afghanistan with the Tornado GR4 and Harrier GR9. No 2 Group has the task of delivering effective combat support to the air component, and is broadly divided into three distinct elements: Air Transport and Air-to-Air Refuelling (AT/AAR); Intelligence, Surveillance, Targeting and Reconnaissance (ISTAR); and Force Protection. The AT/AAR force underpins the United Kingdom's ability to respond rapidly over strategic distance and, once there, to sustain an expeditionary force at range. The provision of accurate and timely intelligence has become an increasingly vital – but scarce – commodity that requires a range of sophisticated capabilities. The RAF is a key contributor to this capability, with platforms such as the Nimrod MR2 and R1, E-3D Sentry, Sentinel R1 and our fast-jet tactical reconnaissance capabilities. In addition, the

Above: A Merlin crewman from No 28(AC) Squadron.

Right: Lossiemouth warriors – a pair of Panavia Tornado GR4s from Nos 12(B) and 14 Squadrons at RAF Lossiemouth.

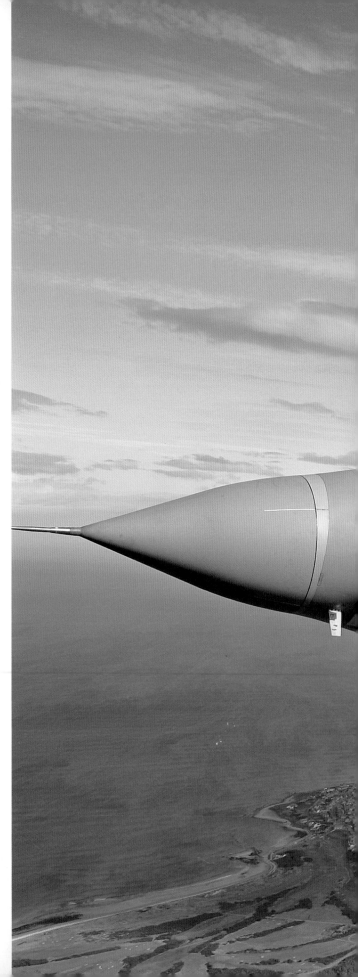

recent procurement of the Reaper Unmanned Air Vehicle (UAV) will significantly enhance the Service's ability to deliver persistent ISTAR. The RAF Regiment, RAF Police and Joint Chemical, Biological, Radiological and Nuclear Regiment stand ready to protect the force at any location around the globe. No 22 Group is the focus for all training in the RAF, from the basic skills given to new recruits, to advanced pilot training and staff training for senior officers. Although increasingly being delivered in conjunction with the other Services, Trenchard's belief that training defines the character and ethos of the Service is still the guiding principle that underpins the RAF's training philosophy.

Operations around the globe have repeatedly demonstrated the vital role that support helicopters play in modern warfare, whether it involves high intensity combat operations or delivering humanitarian relief. Today, the RAF's Chinook, Merlin and Puma helicopters are providing essential battlefield mobility to United Kingdom forces on the ground in Iraq and Afghanistan. These helicopters and their crews operate on a daily basis in some of the most demanding and hostile conditions encountered for many years.

Above: At tree-top level, a Puma HC1 of No 33 Squadron.

Right: A quartet of No 17(R) Squadron Typhoons on the prowl up on high at 40,000ft (13,125m).

On 31 March 2006, the RAF formed nine Expeditionary Air Wings (EAW) at the RAF's main frontline bases of Coningsby, Cottesmore, Kinloss, Leeming, Leuchars, Lossiemouth, Lyneham, Marham and Waddington to support overseas operations. The aim of the Expeditionary Air Wing (EAW) concept was to re-brigade the RAF into a more readily identifiable, high-readiness structure that was trained and prepared for rapid expeditionary deployment. The concept has been successful in delivering a more coherent approach to the RAF's operational training, and has also had significant benefits in improving the cohesiveness of our deployed units.

The Future

The RAF has a long and distinguished history and the role of air power has repeatedly been shown to be vital to the prosecution of military operations. A range of new equipment – including Typhoon, Nimrod MRA4, Sentinel R1, A400M, Future Strategic Tanker Aircraft, Reaper UAV, Joint Strike Fighter – is due to be introduced in the coming years, all of which will enhance the RAF's already formidable frontline capability. This, coupled with one of the best training systems in the world and, of course, a force of highly motivated and professional people, will ensure that the RAF continues to deliver a capability that within the western world is only exceeded by the United States Air Force. New threats, new technologies and new concepts will inevitably present fresh challenges but the RAF is well placed to exploit these opportunities and, in doing so, continue its long tradition for excellence, innovation and professionalism.

Air Chief Marshal Sir Glenn Torpy
Chief of the Air Staff

Above: On the lookout – RAF Typhoons are responsible for protecting UK airspace.

Left: Scramble! A pilot from No 3(F) Squadron charges out to his Eurofighter Typhoon to get airborne in minutes and meet any aerial threats heading towards the UK.

Opposite: A line crewman signals to the aircrew of a Tornado GR4 at the culmination of a training sortie at RAF Marham.

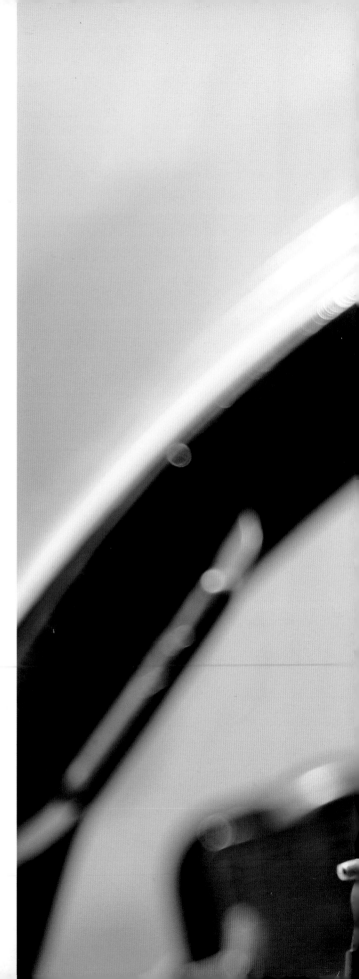

TRAINING FOR THE FUTURE
Preparing for the Challenges Ahead

The men and women of the modern Royal Air Force are serving around the world in some of the most demanding operational environments ever experienced by UK armed forces. New recruits joining the RAF can expect demanding goals to make the grade and prepare them for the front line of operations. They can expect the best possible training and they will be expected to drive for excellence. From pilots to engineers, from medics to the RAF Regiment – the RAF has always prided itself on providing the very best training available and preparing its personnel for the challenges that lie ahead in their military careers.

The RAF College at Cranwell in Lincolnshire is the home of all initial officer training and it is here that the future of the RAF is shaped, with the Station fulfilling a number of key tasks. As well as the College, located here is the Officers and Aircrew Selection Centre, an organisation that interviews and tests the aptitude of applicants who aspire to join the RAF as either ground officers or aircrew. For potential future pilots and weapon systems officers a successful period here opens the door to the RAF and the many careers it offers, but this is only the beginning of a long journey towards joining a front line squadron.

Basic airman and airwoman recruit training takes place at RAF Halton in Buckinghamshire, where new recruits are introduced to RAF life and are taught the skills and knowledge required to enable them to take a full part in support of the front line on operations anywhere in the world. One of the main tenets of Halton is to produce self-reliant and self-motivated personnel who have a sense of pride in, and a responsibility to, the Service.

GETTING THE BASICS

Elementary Flying Training

When young students are selected for RAF pilot training, they embark upon an intensive and carefully structured series of courses – with the very first taste of flying coming either at University Air Squadron (UAS) level or with No 1 Elementary Flying Training School (EFTS) – headquartered at Cranwell. No 1 EFTS is responsible for all initial flying training for the Service

and it includes a Central Flying School (CFS) Grob Tutor squadron, a standards unit, 14 University Air Squadrons (UASs) and the Air Experience Flights (AEFs) that share the UAS assets. The 12 AEFs provide flying experience for young Air Cadets.

The Grob Tutor T1 replaced the venerable Bulldog in 1999 to open the door to flying for young prospective aviators. These aircraft are flown by RAF staff but operated under a civilian contract with VT Aerospace, who supply and service the aircraft. The CFS Tutor Squadron trains both military and civilian contracted instructors for the EFT system, which includes over 60 QFIs (Qualified Flying Instructors) on the UASs.

No 1 EFTS is a relatively new organisation within the RAF that resulted from the disbandment of the Joint Elementary Flying Training School in July 2003. EFT serves to train students to a level that permits a clear, and early, identification of their future potential for further training as new pilots for the front-line squadrons. For a lot of the young aviators who aspire to be the RAF pilots of tomorrow, the UAS is the starting point for learning to fly and for instructors to assess their aptitude. Some 14 UASs operate from 12 stations around the UK, providing a key link between the RAF

Previous pages, left: Engineers provide a vital link in the chain to keep the RAF flying and they receive expert training from the day they join the RAF.

Previous pages, right: The concentration required to fly a fast jet is well illustrated here as ex-Jaguar pilot and experienced Hawk instructor Flt Lt Alex Tennant from No 19(R) Squadron looks hard for his wingman.

Above: With CFS instructor Flt Lt Charlie Brown at the controls, CFS Tutor callsign 'Rustic 2' overflies the famous RAF College Cranwell.

Opposite: Late afternoon winter sun catches a Grob Tutor of No 1 EFTS at RAF Cranwell.

CENTRAL FLYING SCHOOL
Cranwell is the headquarters for the Central Flying School (CFS), which trains flying instructors for their respective aircraft types and is responsible for maintaining standards of excellence for flying training throughout the RAF.

MFTS

The MFTS (Military Flying Training System) concept is due to become reality. MFTS will replace the present flying training arrangements for the RAF, Royal Navy and Army Air Corps with a joint tri-Service programme designed to meet the training requirements of the flying element of the UK front line. MFTS is planned to encompass all flying training from elementary training at UAS level to arrival at the operational conversion unit (OCU) for the designated operational type. The MFTS capability is likely to be achieved through a mix of PFI (Private Finance Initiative) and smart conventional procurement routes.

Above: A UAS student pilot plans his next flight during Elementary Flying Training (EFT).

and the highest calibre of potential new recruits and providing a vital RAF footprint within the University community. University Bursars are officer cadets who receive a bursary on the understanding that they will, on satisfactory completion of their degree studies and UAS training, join the RAF. Students selected as pilots can expect to fly an RAF training syllabus of approximately 60 hours over two years during their degree course. Typically, students fly once a week during term time and during holidays, with the course aimed to teach the basic skills needed to fly an aircraft safely and confidently. The UAS also teaches and streams Direct Entrant students arriving from Initial Officer Training (IOT) at Cranwell. Around 30 per cent of new pilots are school leavers who have completed IOT, with 70 per cent being undergraduates.

The syllabus starts with a basic phase of around ten hours before a period of circuit work. Students then progress to general handling flying, some basic instrument flying and navigation, culminating in a Final Handling Test. RAF EFT at all sites accounts for 60,000 flying hours a year, including the air experience flights given to Air Cadets by the AEFs. Upon completion of the UAS flying course, students are streamed for fast-jet, helicopter or multi-engine training. Successful Direct Entrants will go straight to basic flying training, while University Bursars go to the RAF College for IOT. If the student has made the grade for fast-jet training they head off to RAF Linton-on-Ouse for basic fast-jet training in the Tucano T1. Those streamed for helicopters move to RAF Shawbury and those chosen for multi-engine training attend the MELIN (Multi-Engine Lead In) course before joining No 45(R) Squadron at Cranwell.

Left: The Grob G115 Tutor replaced the Bulldog in RAF service from 1999. The two-seat piston trainer is fully aerobatic and is powered by a 180hp Lycoming 4-cylinder engine, giving it a top speed in level flight of 140kts (161mph) and an endurance of four hours.

Above: Student pilots fly the Tucano T1 to enable them to progress from elementary flying training graduate stage to being prepared for the advanced flying course at Valley on the Hawk.

Opposite: A Tucano T1 of No 76(R) Squadron flown by instructor Flt Lt Jon Dunn and student Fg Off Nick Callinswood performs a break from a No 207(R) Squadron example flown by instructor Flt Lt Keren Watkins and student Fg Off Andy York.

'LINTON'

Basic Fast-Jet Training

A place at RAF Linton-on-Ouse in North Yorkshire is the prize for a graduate who is deemed capable of progressing on to fast-jet aircraft. Here, No 1 Flying Training School (FTS) operates the Shorts Tucano T1 in the Basic Fast Jet Training (BFJT) role. The Tucano is powered by the Garrett TPE331 turbo-prop, which makes it a sprightly performer for the demanding course. Its fighter-like handling characteristics and a tandem cockpit layout make it an ideal platform for

the 120 hours of flying on the course. No 1 FTS is split into two squadrons, Nos 72(R) and 207(R), each having two flights.

Flt Lt Tom Hill is an ex-Tornado F3 pilot and in 2007 was deputy in command at No 207(R) Squadron. "When student pilots arrive at Linton, our job is to take them from the EFT graduate stage with 60 hours of flying experience and prepare them for the advanced flying course at RAF Valley on the Hawk. We start from scratch, teaching them how to fly straight and level, how to fly circuits, how to cope with stalling the aircraft and gradually progress them through the 120 hours of

Above: A pair of Tucanos approach home station RAF Linton-on-Ouse at the culmination of a training flight over the Vale of York.

Right: A No 76(R) Squadron Tucano T1 from the navigation school at Linton-on-Ouse.

flying. They end up being able to lead a pair of Tucanos around a low-level navigation route. They can fly at night and in cloud or bad weather with an instrument rating – operating out of unfamiliar airfields around the country. At the end of the course they get their RAF pilot wings. It's a huge undertaking for a young student and effectively takes them from a PPL-type (Private Pilot's Licence) stage right up to an advanced flying training stage ready for the move to Valley. The navigation phases are very demanding, and a student will typically be preparing the sortie both the night before and early in the morning because of the intense workload. CFS is the agency on the Station that trains new QFIs – ex-front line or 'Creamies' – and also standardises us. Creamies are students that graduate from the course with such flying colours that they are 'creamed off' to stay on as instructors for a further tour on the unit."

The final Tucano sortie on the course is a pairs mission and involves a practice diversion to climb away into a tail chase, which is in effect the beginning of air combat training. The pilots then split off for individual general handling (spinning, stalling, steep turns) before dropping down into low-level to 'hit' a simulated target before returning for circuits back at base – a very challenging sortie. This prepares the student for the big step up to the 420kts (483mph) speed of the Hawk at Valley. Six Tucanos are also based here with No 76(R) Squadron and are used for advanced weapon systems officer training under the organisation formerly known as Tucano Air Navigation School (TANS).

Above: A No 207(R) Squadron Tucano T1 on a training flight from RAF Linton-on-Ouse.

Left: The navigation phases are very demanding and a student will typically be preparing the night before and early in the morning because of the intense workload.

Above: Shorts Tucano T1 on the flightline at Linton-on-Ouse between flights.

Right: Experienced RAF instructors at 'Linton' start from scratch, teaching student pilots how to fly straight and level flight, how to fly circuits and how to cope with stalling the aircraft. They will graduate being able to fly at night and in cloud and bad weather with an instrument rating.

HEADING TO VALLEY

Advanced Fast-Jet Training

Between the craggy peaks of the Cambrian Mountains and Snowdonia a lone black Hawk T1 training jet darts amongst the valleys. The student pilot in the front seat is working harder than ever before, on time and on target, trying to make the grade as a new fighter pilot. The instructor in the back is a hard taskmaster and is carefully monitoring every action as this young pilot learns the skills necessary for the prized cockpit of an RAF fast jet.

On successful completion of the Tucano course, young pilots that have made the grade for advanced fast-jet training move to RAF Valley in Anglesey in North Wales to begin flying the BAE Systems Hawk T1 with No 4 FTS. This training wing has operated the Hawk T1 ever since it entered RAF service in April 1976, being the starting point for the fast-jet training syllabus before students moved on to the weapons phase with the Tactical Weapons Units at either RAF Brawdy or RAF Chivenor. As the two latter stations were closed, the Hawks were consolidated at RAF Valley where the courses are now run by Nos 208(R) and 19(R) Squadrons. In addition to training new pilots, the Hawk is also employed by CFS to train instructors and by No 100 Squadron at RAF Leeming for 'aggressor' duties and fast-jet Weapon Systems Officer (WSO) training as well as Forward Air Controller training with the Joint Forward Air Control and Standards Unit. Perhaps the Hawk's most renowned RAF role is that of the RAF Aerobatic Team, the *Red Arrows*.

Fg Off Ben Durham is a 22-year-old student pilot at No 19(R) Squadron, with his sights firmly set on a fast-jet career on the front line. "I joined the RAF in 2003 at 18 years of age, as a direct entrant from school. Four years later, I am on course TW39 here at Valley having graduated from No 208(R) Squadron across the other side of the airfield. No 208(R) Squadron is the unit that greets you here and it is pretty much a conversion unit for the Hawk when you arrive from Linton. The first half of the No 208(R) course is geared towards

general handling, instrument flying as well as big milestones such as your first Hawk solo flight. You then progress onto navigation and formation training with a 20-hour package of flights. We have all come from a long course on the Tucano and all became very confident handling and operating that type. When you get to the Hawk, it all steps up a gear – we only had 60 flying hours across at '208' and everything happens a lot quicker, but we still have to learn how to navigate with a map, compass and stopwatch."

Above: A student Hawk pilot breaks away from the lead aircraft during formation training.

Opposite: A student fighter pilot's first taste of Hawk T1 flying comes with No 208(R) Squadron at RAF Valley in Anglesey. These two examples are seen during formation training near Cardigan Bay in West Wales.

Above: On the flightline at No 208(R) Squadron.

Right: Hawks from No 208(R) Squadron perform a snap break into the visual circuit pattern as they arrive in the overhead at RAF Valley.

Above: RAF Valley nestles next to the idyllic shoreline and sandy beaches near Rhosnieger on Anglesey.

Following pages: The Hawk nearest the camera has been specially painted to mark the 90th anniversary of No 208(R) Squadron. History and ethos plays a vital part in RAF life.

Right: Low-level flying remains a vital skill for pilots, and there is no margin for error at 400mph! This demanding flying environment is depicted here from the back seat of a Hawk in Wales.

Left: No 19(R) Squadron Hawk T1A radio callsign 'Dervish 1' climbs into the vertical.

Below: Learning to operate a fast jet whilst wearing the helmet, oxygen mask and survival equipment is a key part of training. Here the dark visor disguises the pilot's concentration during a training flight in a Hawk.

Tactical Weapons Training

On graduation from No 208(R) Squadron, pilots move to No 19(R) Squadron across the airfield as qualified Hawk pilots. This unit runs the Tactical Weapons phase of Hawk training, designed to gear the young aviators up ready for the Operational Conversion Unit (OCU) for the particular aircraft they are destined to move to – so here they gain insight into the skills required for the front line. Fg Off Durham continued, "At No 19(R) Squadron we start flying the Hawk with external stores: Carrier Bomb Light Store (CBLS) with practice bombs, a gun and inert missile rounds. We start learning about the gunsight and the weapon systems, learn how to tailchase and how to hold the other aircraft in the gunsight and keep a weapons solution. We then move into the three main phases of the course, which starts with a range phase of strafing and bombing at Pembrey Range in South Wales – working up dual and then going and doing it solo – it's something that everyone looks forward to. Then we move onto an air defence phase, which is basically dynamic raw-handling, but in simulated air combat. For us students it's tough to start with just to hold a good turn rate, but we quickly progress through offensive and defensive fighter manoeuvres and get into 2v1 fights with instructors and conduct practice intercepts. Then we move into the ground attack phase, which culminates in simulated attack profiles (SAPs). This is where the instructors will give us prioritised targets and an intelligence scenario

for us to execute a fully integrated mission. We do about 15 SAPs, working to a time on target plus or minus five seconds – so you need to be on your game to get there! We culminate with the 'Op Phase', which involves effectively running a mini-war where we need to apply everything we have learned, including low-level evasion, air combat and then getting back on track to hit the target. We do all of this in just 40 hours of flying at No 19(R) Squadron. It's a high workload and as a duty student we will expect to be in at 0630, maybe fly twice during the day, get back for dinner, hit the gym, before getting our head in the books for a few hours before bed and then up again first thing the next morning. It's a tough course that takes a lot of commitment and we all find it challenging but extremely rewarding. It's hard work but it's everything I could have wanted to have

Above: The busy Hawk flightline at No 19(R) Squadron, RAF Valley. The aircraft are serviced and maintained by civilian contractors.

Opposite: A Hawk T1A of No 19(R) Squadron equipped with AIM-9 Sidewinder missile acquisition training rounds dives dramatically during air combat training in the Tactical Weapons phase of the course at RAF Valley.

Right: A student pilots walks to his Hawk T1A for a low-level training simulated attack mission in the local North Wales military training area (MTA).

achieved. The future for a student is bright here on 19(R) Squadron. Whatever front line role awaits us, they all have an interesting and important part to play in UK operations around the world. Whether it be Typhoon, Harrier, or either Tornado variant, they are all very capable platforms and I am really looking forward to having the opportunity to operate one of them".

Wg Cdr Adrian Hill is officer commanding No 19(R) Squadron. "Our course is constantly evolving and most recently there has been a huge change in terms of what we are teaching – more in line with what is required by the front line. We got together with the OCUs and devised new ways to improve the skills of the ab initio students that we output. We did very little medium level work in the past and our air combat profiles were a little bit archaic. So we reviewed the syllabus and moved sorties around to put flying hours to better use. We have now introduced two sorties to give students a taste of medium level air interdiction and close air support (CAS). This gives the student a look at flying around at 15,000ft in a wagon wheel over the target as opposed to thundering over at 250ft – which they still need to do, however, and we still devote 10 hours to low-level flying to teach these basic, but essential, skills of the fighter pilot. We have moved the air defence phase that used to take up a lot of airborne time to the simulator. We teach Combat Air Patrol (CAP) procedures and short-range commits off the CAP so they will get a pop-up intercept and pick it up with a ground controlled intercept to visually identify or engage a target if it's deemed hostile. We also now train using Typhoon and Tornado F3 standard voice communications – so we are streamlining to dovetail with future training. This is ultimately planned as a move to ease our transition to the new Hawk Mk128."

On 30 July 2003 the BAE Systems Hawk Mk128 was selected as the next-generation RAF Advanced Jet Trainer. The arrival of the new Hawks for the tactical weapons phase of training will herald a massive boost in training capability. Wg Cdr Hill: "The Mk128 will start arriving here at Valley in 2008 and we expect IOC (Initial Operational Capability) in 2009 and FOC (Full

Above and top: In the office – a student from No 19(R) Squadron in a Hawk T1A.

Left: Before every flight the aircrew perform an external visual 'walk round' check of the aircraft to ensure no detail has been overlooked.

Operational Capability) towards the end of 2010 – this milestone being marked by the first ab initio course flying fast-jet tactical weapons training with the new aircraft. We are trying to prepare ourselves as well as possible now, but without the actual aircraft. The only advanced 'kit' we have in the Hawk T1 is a GPS – so we are teaching how to navigate with this. In the Mk128 we will have synthetic radar, embedded simulation training equipment, and we will ultimately move away from paper planning and maps towards computer aided planning – the same software as the front line uses. I expect No 208(R) Squadron to initially run a bridging course with the Hawk T1 to smooth the process from the Tucano to the Mk128, with the eventual plan being for a new basic trainer to arrive from 2015 under MFTS." The RAF fast-jet training programme is also looking to increase the output of single-seat capable pilots. "The current front-line breakdown is that two thirds of the pilots from here go to two-seat slots, i.e. Tornados. When Typhoon ramps up and the Harrier is replaced by the Joint Combat Aircraft (JCA), the pilot ratio will become 50-55% going to single seat – so we need to raise the output standard so that double the amount produced are single-seat standard."

Above: Breaking for action – this No 19(R) Squadron Hawk T1A shows off its top surface as it breaks hard to begin air-combat training with its captive carry AIM-9 Sidewinder missile acquisition training rounds.

Left: With the Lleyn Peninsula in the background, a No 19(R) Squadron Hawk T1A, radio callsign 'Dervish 1', cruises towards Snowdonia on a crystal clear day, perfect for flying training.

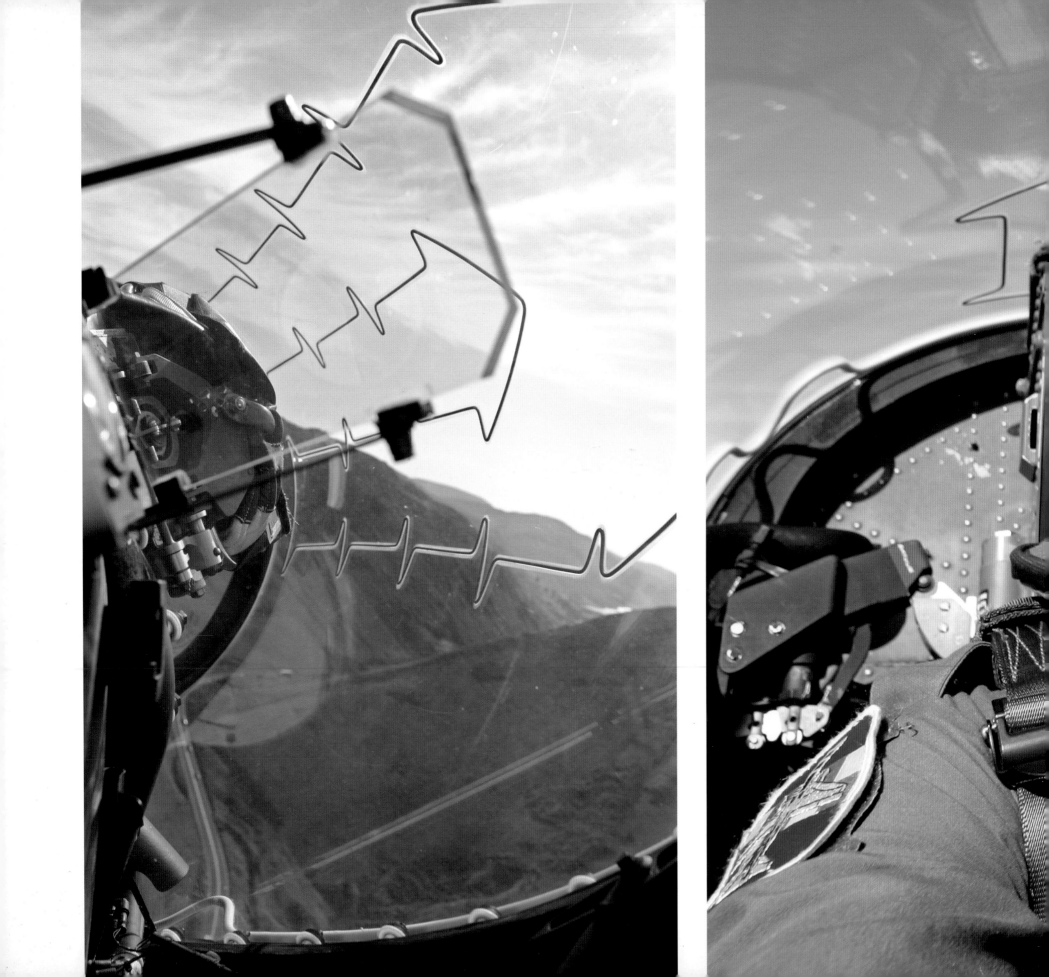

Previous pages, left: Low-level flying allows pilots to avoid enemy radar with terrain masking. Here a Hawk descends into the 'Machynlleth Loop', a well-known series of remote valleys in North Wales that are valuable for such training. Note the Miniature Detonating Cord (MDC) in the Perspex that would shatter the canopy in the event of an emergency and ejection.

Previous pages, right: Fast-jet pilots are taught close formation training from an early stage as it is a core competency.

Right: Rounding the picturesque bays on North Wales' coastline, a No 19(R) Squadron Hawk T1A heads back to RAF Valley.

Following pages, left: Pulling hard – a Hawk T1A of No 19(R) Squadron gets into a turning fight in air combat training.

Following pages, right: The future – a BAE Systems Hawk Advanced Jet Trainer breaks away from a current RAF Hawk T1A. The RAF selected the Hawk Mk128 in 2003 as the replacement for the T1 variant in the tactical weapons phase of training and its arrival will herald a massive boost in training capability.

MULTI-SKILLED

Training For The Heavies

Pilot training is not all about the fast-jet community. As well as training for the RAF's helicopter force (detailed in Chapter Five), the RAF also trains for its diverse force of multi-engine heavy aircraft. No 3 Flying Training School (3 FTS) at RAF Cranwell operates two highly important units that prepare students for the heavier end of the RAF aircraft spectrum. No 45(R) Squadron conducts multi-engine training with a fleet of seven King Air B200s, riding alongside No 55(R) Squadron flying the Dominie T1 for WSO and NCO (Non-Commissioned Officer) aircrew training.

For those pilots selected to fly the RAF's larger, multi-engine types, the road from EFT starts with a spell at Cranwell's MELIN multi-engine 'lead-in' training flight and the Slingsby Firefly T67M-260 with a three-bladed prop power plant. This is followed by a course with No 45(R) Squadron on the King Air, a type that replaced its predecessor Jetstream T1s of the Multi-Engine Training Squadron in March 2004.

Flt Lt Leo Cheng is a 24-year-old student who graduated at 45(R) in summer 2007. "I started RAF flying in summer 2001 with the University of West England in Bristol on an RAF bursary. I joined Bristol UAS and did my EFT there before starting initial officer training at Cranwell in 2004. The flying courses at Cranwell take about a year, starting with MELIN and then moving on to the King Air. The King Air is a big step up from the MELIN Firefly with its two engines, retractable undercarriage and semi-glass cockpit. There were six guys on my course and we have a maximum of three courses on the go at any one time, split between A and B flights – the basic phase and the advanced phase. I am so pleased to have graduated and I am hoping to be selected to fly the C-130 Hercules."

Officer commanding No 45(R) Squadron is Sqn Ldr Jad Reece, an ex-Nimrod pilot with a wealth of experience. "We train all the multi-engine pilots ready to join the OCUs for all the fleets, everything from Hercules, to VC10, E-3D, C-17 and now the new

Sentinel R1 ISTAR aircraft. The Squadron is actually in its 91st year and our normal strength is around 20 QFIs and about 40 students on the course at any given time. These range from ab initio students selected for multi-engine training to those that have been to fast-jet or rotary flying training and been re-streamed to us. So we run 5-6 different courses here but our student output standard is to the same level. Our student pilots leave here having received their RAF wings on a multi-engine aircraft and are ready to join a type OCU. Our seven King Air 200s are owned privately and leased to Serco and they sub-contract to us – it's a real success story and we work together as an excellent team. The King Air is superb for our training role. The avionics configuration is ideal for preparing pilots for the front line types in the RAF as we have a mix of some glass-cockpit elements and analogue instruments."

Clearly the multi-engine crews need to be prepared to operate around the world, such is the tempo and diversity of modern RAF operations. Sqn Ldr Reece continued, "Our students all fly an overseas training flight – they need experience of going overseas. We get to travel all over Europe and we try to vary the routes as it helps keep instructors current. In addition, some of the OCUs that we feed students into support tactical and low-level training elements – such as the Hercules – so we teach this as a core pilot skill. Our course culminates in simulated mission profiles and we will put together a mission to go to an airfield with several simulated emergencies. We also get the students to fly in the busiest of airways, with extra injects such as an unplanned diversion before getting back here safely."

Left: Sceptre formation – a mixed flight of No 45(R) Squadron King Air B200s and No 55(R) Squadron Dominie T1s head out from home station RAF Cranwell.

Mission Specialists

Training at Cranwell is not just about pilots. No 55(R) Squadron operates the jet black 1965 vintage HS Dominie T1 to train WSOs and Non-Commissioned Weapon Systems Operators (WSOps) prior to joining the front line. All WSO flying training starts with a short 'elementary' phase conducted by a dedicated team of instructors at the Initial Navigation Training Section of 55(R) Squadron, using Tutor aircraft from 1 Squadron, 1 EFTS. Flt Lt Mal Prissick is a Dominie captain; he actually left the RAF as an Air Commodore in 2001 having been the Commandant of CFS and Station Commander at RAF Marham. Flt Lt Prissick has been at 55(R) Squadron ever since and holds a reserve commission. "The RAF was running short of pilots and changed a number of posts to reserve commissioned officers. Of the 14 pilots here on the unit four are reservists. This frees up younger officers to fill the important front-line slots. We train WSOs for respective aircraft types, both multi-engine and fast jet – but the latter is a diminishing role as our only fast-jet type that operates with a WSO now is the Tornado.

Consequently, the emphasis is moving away from fast-jet WSO training towards WSOp training. These students have a generic course to learn the skills of mission operators as well as synthetic simulator training. They learn how to operate our systems in the back of the Dominie as a precursor to the type they will progress to on the front line. The WSOp courses take between nine months and a year with graduating students moving on to the front line as Rotary-wing Crewmen, Multi-Engine Crewmen, Sensor Operators or Linguists. Those WSOs headed for the Tornado move from here to a course on the Hawk at No 100 Squadron at RAF Leeming for a fast-jet slant before their OCU. We also have WSO and WSOp maritime flying training for the Nimrod, which sees us training down at 500ft over the sea." A large and flexible Squadron, all aircrew other than pilots are trained on 55(R) Squadron.

Above: Sqn Ldr Jad Reece, Officer Commanding No 45(R) Squadron, and Flt Lt Neil Cottle in a King Air B200 break from Flt Lt Mal Prissick and Sqn Ldr Craig Daykin in a Dominie T1.

Above left: No 45(R) Squadron conducts multi-engine training with a fleet of seven King Air B200s.

RAF FLYING CLUBS

Although most people think of flying in the RAF as being the preserve of those who have joined up as full-time aircrew, in fact there is a thriving community of other trades who take advantage of the RAF Flying Clubs to follow their passion for active aviation. The RAF Flying Clubs are open to all members of the military, reserves and cadet organisations, as well as selected civilians. They have a wide range of aircraft available for hire at very low rates and offer pleasure flights, flying licences and competitive flying such as precision piloting or sport aerobatics. Most large stations have a flying club to ensure you can be a pilot in the RAF even if you didn't join as one!

TRAINING THE ENGINEERS

Defence College of Aeronautical Engineering

Despite much of the ground support for flying training being contracted out, the RAF still relies on training its own engineers to support front-line assets. These highly skilled and important personnel underpin a squadron, ensuring that aircraft are ready every day to meet operational needs. The Defence College of Aeronautical Engineering (DCAE) was established on 1 April 2004 and was an important step in the migration of all three Services to a tri-Service Defence Training System. The federated College, with its headquarters at Cosford in Shropshire, provides training for all three Services across five different sites: DCAE (Gosport), DCAE (Arborfield), DCAE (Cosford), DCAE (Cranwell) and DCAE (St Athan).

The principal task of the DCAE is to provide high quality, relevant and up-to-date aeronautical engineering training to fulfil the needs of tomorrow's front line. It meets this aim by providing initial specialist training to prepare Service personnel for their first employment, subsequently followed by advanced training to give aeronautical technicians an increased skill and responsibility base to meet their career aspirations and advance their professional development.

The bulk of the RAF's engineering training takes place at No1 SofTT (School of Technical Training). Primarily based at Cosford, No 1 SofTT consists of Aerosystems Training Wing (ATW) and Military Training Wing (MTW). ATW focuses on the planning and delivery of aeronautical engineering training to aircraft mechanical and avionic multi-skilled mechanics and technicians, weapon technicians, survival equipment fitters, and aircraft painters and finishers. In addition, it delivers Trade Management Training for RAF Junior and Senior Non-Commissioned Officers and Expedient Repair Training to No 1 SofTT and to the wider RAF. ATW provides an extensive range of courses and trains over 5000 students annually via its various training squadrons. It also runs a Foundation Degree course for ab initio Engineering Officers.

MTW concentrates on delivering physical education and personal development training as well as meeting the welfare, pastoral and ethos needs of the trainees while in No 1 SofTT. In addition, it delivers military skills training and force development training for both trainees and permanent staff alike. The decision to implement a discrete split in the responsibility for the management of training delivery, and trainee management, has stemmed from the combined needs to deliver multi-skilling in the aircraft engineering trades and the focused delivery of essential warfighting skills to prepare the trainees for operational deployments.

As part of the Defence Training Review programme a Public Private Partnership route has been chosen for the delivery of a Defence Training Academy, of which the DCAE would be one element. It is proposed that DCAE will move to a newly built Defence Academy at MoD St Athan, South Wales. However, no significant moves are currently anticipated before 2011. Moreover, other units currently based at Cosford are likely to be relocated, but as yet no decisions about such moves have been made.

Above left: In the hot seat – DCAE Cosford's Specialist Training School provides hands-on tuition from day one.

Photograph: Crown Copyright

BASIC RECRUIT TRAINING

Heading to Halton

Recruit training may have changed in many ways since the RAF was established in 1918 but the aim has remained constant throughout: to produce high quality individuals ready to go on to further training with a solid foundation of core values that will see them through their careers. While the nature of recruit training has developed in many respects over the years to reflect the modern environment, it is still challenging and has increased in both course length and in its emphasis on field skills, with recruits leaving basic training more ready than the previous generations for life in an expeditionary air force.

Basic Training, or Phase One training as it is known, takes place at RAF Halton under the auspices of the Recruit Training Squadron (RTS), part of the Station's Training Wing. The RTS syllabus is split into three modules. The Induction module deals with the transition from civilian to military life and introduces the basic skills required to serve in the Royal Air Force. The Ground Defence Training, or 'Green' module, follows, in which recruits are instructed in the basics of Chemical, Biological, Radiological and Nuclear warfare, first aid, skill-at-arms and field living, all culminating in a four-day exercise. Finally, comes the 'Blue' module, so called because the recruits wear the RAF blue uniform for the first time, in which the emphasis is concentrated on developing team-working skills and preparing for the formal Graduation Parade. From arrival to graduation the Basic Recruit Course lasts 64 days.

To deliver the syllabus the RTS has six separate training teams, each responsible for an intake. Each team consists of a Flight Lieutenant, two Sergeants and six Corporals. The team provides not only the pastoral care for recruits but also instruction in General Service Knowledge, General Service Training and Drill.

Instructors on the RTS are drawn from a wide variety of trades and backgrounds. This is intentional, to bring a wide breadth of experience to the training environment – there are currently more than 17

separate trades represented amongst the instructional staff. This also allows recruits to meet members of their chosen trade before going on to professional training themselves and is a crucial part of the learning process, enabling instructors to dispel myths and give guidance for the future.

Recruit welfare is an area where significant developments have been made and is an area that continues to improve. Recruits have access to an internet suite, a cinema, the New Comers Club, and this year will see the opening of 'The Roundel', a totally new welfare facility for recruits to use in their spare time. All recruits have access to members of the chaplaincy centre and a recent innovation was to introduce Welfare and Support Personnel known as 'Wasps'. These are NCOs who wear civilian clothes and whose purpose is to provide the recruits with a more informal environment to discuss

problems. Any recruit who suffers an injury or has failed to pass an element of training will remain on RTS, but will transfer to the Recruit Development Flight until they are ready to rejoin mainstream training.

It is clear that recruit training has changed in many ways, but it is important to see that there are also many areas of continuity. The aim has always been to produce individuals able to succeed within the RAF and provide them with the basic tools to become tomorrow's leaders. Recruits still start their careers with a haircut; drill instructors are still imposing figures; and the Graduation Parade is still one of the most memorable moments in their career.

Above: Team building is an important element of the course at the Recruit Training Squadron at RAF Halton.

Opposite: Recruit Training Squadron students preparing for their Graduation Parade – one of the most memorable moments of their career.

Above: For recruits, training exercise 'Blue Warrior' is a key phase and is designed to be a representative peacekeeping situation that includes routine patrols, manning vehicle checkpoints and administrating themselves in the field.

Left: Recruits' Ground Defence Training (RGDT) is run by the RAF Regiment and teaches recruits basic soldiering skills that culminates in an exercise away from RAF Halton. The first aspect taught is Chemical, Biological, Radiological and Nuclear warfare skills.

Photographs above and opposite: Crown Copyright.

TESTING FOR THE FUTURE

Learn To Test – Test To Learn

At Boscombe Down in Wiltshire lies one of the most influential flying stations in the UK. It is here that much of the developmental test work for the RAF is conducted by ace test pilots at the Aircraft Test and Evaluation Centre (ATEC). These pilots are the modern-day equivalent of famous names such as Peter Twiss, Eric 'Winkle' Brown and John Farley, although arguably today's flying is conducted with far lower levels of risk than the early days of flight testing.

Dave Southwood is a hugely experienced test pilot and a famous name at Boscombe. "You can think of flight testing in two main areas today. Firstly you have the performance and flying qualities side and secondly you have the systems for navigation and attack. We are now operating in a world of sophisticated computers and simulators and industry now develops advanced mathematical models for new aeroplane designs. They will assimilate these in a simulator and conduct much of the flying qualities and performance development work there. So when you go out and test fly the aeroplane for real, the profile is geared towards validating what you found in the simulator – but you will always find differences. The flight test data is then used to refine the model in the simulator. So the importance of flight testing is still there and always will be, because you can't remove the predictability out of a simulator.

The advance of more complex avionics systems and the integration of precision-guided munitions has radically changed testing. I remember the first trials I did in the Jaguar involved clearing American Mk82 bombs for the jet. We took the bomb and put it on the jet and then looked at the ballistics. We really just wanted to ensure it separated cleanly from the aeroplane. That was it! Now you have all the feeds from the main computer and the avionics system to integrate with the weapon. It is far more complex."

Flt Lt Jez Robinson is one of the newest RAF pilots chosen to test future capabilities as a student on the 2007 Empire Test Pilots' School (ETPS) course here.

"I first applied to ETPS just after I had completed my first Tornado GR4 tour. I didn't really have an expectation to get in and I didn't, so I re-applied later and here I am. I am 37 years old and the youngest pilot this year is a Harrier pilot who is 32. They choose test pilots by looking at projected requirements for the next two to three years and recruit on a type-specific basis for each aircraft in the inventory. This is one course and it runs from January to the end of December and is split into three terms. The first four weeks are pure ground school; this is hard work, lots of mathematics and mechanics. I covered things that I did in two years at University in just four weeks! Then we start flying and getting cleared solo on the school's Hawks and Alpha Jets, with the Tucano coming a bit later followed by the heavy aircraft such as the BAC 1-11."

The ETPS course boasts a famously heavy workload for the students. "During ground school we start our first tests, which are cockpit assessments. We usually reckon on two or three hours of testing followed by 30-40 hours writing up the test results – ten hours of writing for each hour of testing. On airborne tasks our aircraft are specially instrumented and so we download onto the computer to spend literally hundreds of hours poring over graphs to get the right data. For every test flight we fly, we prepare a flight test plan where we write up exactly what we are going to do, then we have our test cards checked and signed off before we go and fly the sortie. After the sortie we have 48 hours to complete a post-flight report; for a full report we get ten days to write it up, which includes one day off a weekend. Normally we will be writing one test report whilst flying another and preparing a third. So we usually have two or three on the go as per the syllabus. But it's great! Last month I flew ten different aircraft types, from gliders to the Extra 300. I was in France last month spinning Alpha Jets, and then went to Sweden to fly the Gripen."

Left: A unique ETPS asset, the School's Harvard is prepared for a
handling test sortie from Boscombe Down.

Rhys Williams is another highly experienced instructor at ETPS. "We are instructing both test pilots and flight test engineers, so a lot of what we teach is about systems. We make good use of other assets at flight test stations such as the US Navy NP-3 Orion flying classroom that is based at Patuxent River, MD. A lot of our radar work is now conducted on the Saab JAS-39 Gripen in Sweden. We simply cannot afford to run all aircraft types in house, so we use the Gripen as our sophisticated front-line aircraft as it is a high-thrust, high-performance supersonic fighter with great avionics systems. Two of our major assets here at Boscombe are the Beagle Basset and ASTRA Hawk, both of which feature digital fly-by-wire variable stability controls and are a highly sought after indigenous capability. At Boscombe we are looking at highly advanced technology through a combination of ATEC and QinetiQ and we use some unique aircraft."

Indeed, the teams at Boscombe are playing key roles in a number of major new programmes such as the F-35 Joint Combat Aircraft (JCA) that will replace the Harrier from the middle of the next decade. The Tornado Integrated Avionics Research Aircraft (TIARA) is testing flying helmet technology that allows pilots to project target data directly into their field of vision as well as to look through the cockpit floor! One of the most exceptional aircraft is the vectored-thrust aircraft advanced flight control (VAAC) Harrier, which is operated through the joint US-UK Joint Strike Fighter (JSF) office and uses advanced fly-by-wire technology to refine the proposed control attributes of the F-35.

Left: The last first-generation Harrier still flying in the Northern Hemisphere, flown here by test pilot Lt Chris Gotke. This is the vectored-thrust aircraft advanced flight control (VAAC) Harrier. As with all Harriers, four movable nozzles on the Pegasus engine allow the pilot to vector the thrust from the engine to facilitate hovering the aircraft as well as conventional forward flight.

FIGHTER SQUADRON
Fast Jets

It is a damp early morning in a remote corner of Lincolnshire and the air hangs heavy as the weak winter sun tries to break through the layer of leaden cloud. In the distance, a dull roar builds and in no time a pair of dart-like fast jets hurtle skyward into the gloom, heading out to challenge their marauding prey. RAF Coningsby in Lincolnshire is the home of the No 121 Expeditionary Air Wing (EAW) and the RAF's latest and greatest swing-role jet fighter – the Eurofighter Typhoon and its new generation of RAF combat aces.

STORM FORCE

Eurofighter Typhoon

The Typhoon may have been a while coming, but it's a force to be reckoned with. An RAF fighter pilot and a Typhoon is more impressive than James Bond and his Aston Martin DBS. It is an aircraft that delivers an immediate and uncompromising response to anyone that tries to challenge it. Every Typhoon pilot you talk to says "the performance is blistering". It has been likened to the English Electric Lightning in terms of its prowess, with an awesome thrust-to-weight ratio and boasting a formidable ability to roar to 36,000ft (10,970m) in under two minutes from brakes off. Most Typhoon pilots see other fighter types as 'easy meat' in a turning fight and as a newly introduced weapons platform it clearly has huge growth potential.

Built by the four-nation Eurofighter GmbH consortium, the EPCs (Eurofighter Partner Companies) comprise BAE Systems from the UK, EADS from Germany and Spain and Alenia from Italy. This cutting-edge fighter is currently at the very beginning of its operational life, with capabilities being examined and expanded as its future is shaped. It is destined to form the backbone of the RAF fighter force well into the future.

RAF Coningsby is now becoming the spiritual home of RAF Typhoon operations, with no less than four Typhoon units to be based here. These are namely No 17(R) Squadron, the Typhoon Operational Evaluation Unit (OEU), No 29(R) Squadron, the Operational Conversion Unit (OCU), and two front line units, Nos 3(F) and XI(F) Squadrons. The RAF's largest Typhoon

squadron is the OCU, No 29(R) Squadron, which is responsible for the technical and tactical training of all engineers and pilots for the RAF Typhoon force supporting the front-line squadrons. Typhoon represents a huge step forward in technology for the Royal Air Force and is planned to fill both air defence and ground attack roles for the RAF. It is capable of switching between the two roles whilst in flight, thus making it a true swing-role, as opposed to multi-role, fighter. The RAF is making it as effective as possible, as quickly as possible.

Right: No 17(R) Squadron is the Typhoon Operational Evaluation Unit (OEU) and is based at RAF Coningsby. Here its Officer Commanding, Wg Cdr Toby Craig, dramatically breaks his Typhoon F2 towards the camera.

Opposite: The awesome performance of Typhoon FGR4 is shown to good effect as the aircraft totes an impressive weapons fit of Paveway II precision bombs, AIM-120 AMRAAM and AIM-132 ASRAAM missiles.

Previous pages, left: Action at RAF Coningsby. An instructor pilot from the Typhoon OCU straps in as a pair of the fighters break overhead on return from a training mission.

Previous pages, right: Bristling with 1,000lb Paveway II precision bombs, AIM-120 Advanced Medium Range Air-to-Air Missiles (AMRAAM) and AIM-132 ASRAAM short-range missiles, this is the swing-role Eurofighter Typhoon FGR4.

Above: Flown by Sqn Ldr Graham Pemberton, this Eurofighter Typhoon FGR4 is from No 17(R) Squadron, the Typhoon OEU.

Left: A fine head-on study of a Typhoon F2 of No 29(R) Squadron, the Typhoon Operational Conversion Unit (OCU) from RAF Coningsby, flown by Flt Lt Antony Parkinson. Initial production Typhoons, capable of employment in the air defence role only, are known as Typhoon T1 for the two-seat variant, and Typhoon F2 for the single-seat variant. New 'mark' numbers have now been assigned to both single-seat and twin-seat Typhoons which have been upgraded or built new to so-called Block 5 standard, which adds air-to-surface capabilities. The Block 5 two-seater is now known as the Typhoon T3 and the single-seater is known as the Typhoon FGR4 (denoting Fighter, Ground Attack and Reconnaissance).

Typhoon Technical

The RAF has a requirement for a total of 232 Typhoons to be delivered in three Tranches. The initial Tranche of 55 aircraft includes three differing build standards of Typhoon: Block 1, Block 2 and Block 5. The Typhoon airframe is clearly in a league of its own in relation to other RAF types. It is agile, powerful, has incredible acceleration, can out-turn all the current threats and has an excellent high-altitude performance envelope, which means that a pilot can sit at high level using the full potential of the aircraft systems. Initial preparation for entry into RAF service was completed under the 'Case White' programme at BAE Systems' Warton facility in Lancashire.

In July 2007 the RAF Typhoon Force reached Quick Reaction Alert (QRA) OED (Operational Employment Date) when Nos 3(F) and XI(F) Squadrons assumed rotational responsibility for this vital air defence role, with 3(F) as the lead squadron. This will be followed by the all-weather fighter (ADX) OED in early 2008. The force is then looking towards multi-role (air-to-surface capability) OED later in 2008. The RAF is keen to introduce the important air-to-surface capabilities of Typhoon as soon as operationally viable. Therefore, from Block 5 of Tranche 1 this capability is planned to be introduced and will be retrofitted across the fleet of earlier aircraft. The attack capability will initially involve the integration of the Litening III laser designator pod and the Enhanced Paveway II GPS/laser-guided bombs, both of which are proven systems, to give the type a strong and reliable capability in this field.

Opposite: Turning and burning. Even with a full heavy load, the Typhoon is an agile performer. Here Sqn Ldr Graham Pemberton selects full reheat from the impressive Eurojet EJ200 engines and heaves the jet into a tight left-hand turn. The Typhoon is very powerful and boasts incredible acceleration. It can also out-manoeuvre most other fighters it is likely to encounter.

Above: Typhoon pilot Flt Lt Andy Millikin in the office. The advanced anti-G suit worn by Typhoon aircrew offers incredible tolerance against the demands of air combat.

Above: Emerging from its Hardened Aircraft Shelter (HAS) a No 3(F) Squadron Typhoon F2 is scrambled to meet an incoming threat to UK airspace.

Right: The RAF has a requirement for 232 Typhoons that will be built and delivered in three Tranches. Tranche 1 is now complete and includes 55 Typhoons that were built to three incremental standards; Block 1, Block 2 and the multi-role capable Block 5.

Typhoon Force

Wg Cdr Lol Bennett is OC No 3(F) Squadron, which was the RAF's first front line Typhoon unit. "I was a Tornado GR1 pilot and completed tours on Nos 617 and XV(R) Squadrons as a Qualified Weapons Instructor (QWI), after which I went out to the USA and undertook an exchange tour at NAS Lemoore on F/A-18s for four years single-seat multi-role flying. On my return I joined the Typhoon IPT (Integrated Project Team) as requirements manager before I went to staff college. I was then promoted and moved into this job. The Squadron stood up as a Typhoon unit on 31 March 2006 and actually transitioned that day from 34 years of Harrier flying to the Typhoon. At that time we had just two aircraft, one pilot had finished the OCU, I was still a student going through the course with another three of my pilots, and we had about 45 engineers working embedded within the OCU. Since then the Squadron has grown on a weekly basis with aircraft, pilots and engineers and in the middle of June 2006 we set up our own engineering department. In the middle of July we

moved over to this HAS (Hardened Aircraft Shelter) site and moved into fully autonomous operations. I now have a full establishment of 16 pilots, including four ab initios and an American exchange officer, and about 130 of 138 engineers and 11 jets. Twelve of the pilots are currently combat ready in the air defence role." Within a year of this stand-up in late February 2007 the Squadron conducted its first live-firing exercise with a number of MBDA ASRAAM missiles fired on the Aberporth range.

The first significant operational milestone for No 3(F) Squadron was starting Quick Reaction Alert duty from the middle of 2007. Wg Cdr Bennett: "Everyone from the station commander to the newest pilots on the type will stand QRA. We are already looking towards the end of 2008 in terms of our mission and our focus is very much on achieving a multi-role capability. The

way it will work is that 3(F) is the lead squadron for ADX and QRA and XI(F) is the lead for the multi-role aspect. What this means is that the focal point of contact for those roles is 3(F) and XI(F) respectively, but essentially we are doing everything together. For me it is also about looking forward to our participation in operations and looking back at history to learn lessons. I am keen for my pilots to read old WW2 accounts from Typhoon pilots that back in 1943 were strafing trains and dropping 500lb bombs having flown over the coast at 30ft in poor weather. We are really starting to deliver the aircraft's potential now. One of my flight commanders on the unit was one of the early individuals to fly the Block 50 F-16 and will routinely say he would rather go to war tomorrow in Typhoon because of the massive advantages in what the aircraft can do above other F-jet platforms".

Above: Lined up on runway 25 at Coningsby – with an awesome thrust-to-weight ratio a Typhoon can roar to 36,000ft (10,970m) in under two minutes from brakes off.

Right: In July 2007 the RAF Typhoon Force reached Quick Reaction Alert (QRA) OED (Operational Employment Date) when Nos 3(F) and XI(F) Squadrons assumed rotational responsibility for this role, with 3(F) as the lead squadron.
Photograph by Geoffrey H. Lee

Following pages, left: Low December light contrasts three Typhoon F2s on patrol in the contrails up at 40,000ft (12,190m) over the North Sea.

Following pages, right: A No 29(R) Squadron Typhoon T1 catches the golden autumn evening light as it is prepared for night flying training.

Eagles in Action

No XI(F) Squadron, whose motto is 'Swifter and Keener than Eagles', is the lead squadron for the multi-role element of operations for the Typhoon Force. OC No XI(F) Squadron is Wg Cdr Gav Parker: "As the lead multi-role squadron our efforts are very much focussed on delivering a flexible and potent air-to-surface capability to complement the aircraft's already exceptional air-to-air performance. We have now completed our air defence work-up, and with the arrival of the Block 5 Typhoon FGR4 aircraft standard, which is capable of conducting multi- and swing-role missions, our training has shifted to match the incremental delivery of a variety of air-to-surface weapons and capabilities. Our ex-Jaguar and Harrier pilots, many of whom have also had experience flying the F-16 and the F-18, all say that Typhoon has excellent potential as an air-to-surface platform. Heavy weapons training exercises flown in the UK's air weapons ranges and close-air-support (CAS) exercises flown with the British Army have shown that its combination of range, persistence and payload will make it a formidable CAS aircraft. Its navigational systems and cockpit layout allow pilots to rapidly locate and identify targets, it is very stable and cool in the dive, and its power and agility allow it to deliver weapons quickly and accurately without having to spend too long in the threat band."

Above right: Armourers from No XI(F) Squadron load Paveway II laser-guided bombs onto a Typhoon.

Left: 'Swifter and Keener than Eagles', No XI(F) Squadron is commanded by Wg Cdr Gav Parker and is the RAF's lead operational unit for the multi-role Typhoon FGR4.

Following pages, left: Man and machine – Flt Lt Etienne Smith and Eurofighter Typhoon FGR4.

Following pages, right: The RAF is keen to introduce the important air-to-surface capabilities of Typhoon as soon as operationally viable. The ground-attack capability will initially involve the integration of the Litening III laser designator pod (LDP) and the Enhanced Paveway II (EPW2) GPS/laser-guided bombs, proven systems to give the type a strong and reliable initial capability in this field.

Supporting The Front Line

No 17(R) Squadron is arguably one of the most significant Typhoon units as it is the Typhoon Operational Evaluation Unit (OEU). Commanded by Wg Cdr Toby Craig, an ex-Jaguar pilot with a wealth of experience in a number of roles, this specialist unit is responsible for bringing the latest capabilities of the Typhoon into service for the front line. "We have been and remain at the forefront of RAF Typhoon operations since it came into service. No 17(R) Squadron is part of the RAF's Air Warfare Centre (AWC), which is different to the other units on the Station as they are assigned to No 1 Group. Typhoon is a phenomenal aeroplane to fly, with outstanding performance and incredible potential. At this Squadron we are responsible for driving forward operational capability for Typhoon. The Squadron is primarily responsible for aircraft capability, with our sister units Nos 29(R), No 3(F) and No XI(F) Squadrons being responsible for the delivery of that capability and for the training of both aircrew and engineers. This aeroplane isn't just about pilots: it's also about all the support that is behind it. The way the technology allows us to evolve has radically changed the RAF. Our role on the Squadron is primarily to take the product as delivered from industry, see if it does what it says on the tin, prove the delivered capability and provide

operational advice to the front line about how to operate the equipment."

In 2007 No 17(R) Squadron embarked on a period of heavy weapons load trials geared towards multi-role capability with a series of trials sorties with its Block 5 Typhoon FGR4s to test a very impressive weapons load of no less than six Paveway II laser-guided bombs, four AIM-120 AMRAAM missiles and two AIM-132 ASRAAM short-range missiles. Squadron pilot Sqn Ldr Graham Pemberton: "A large focus of our work here on the OEU at the moment is geared towards the multi-role OED. This current trial sees us flying a selection of Paveway II precision bombs, two of which are instrumented, and is part of the weapons clearance process for the MoD, with the fit having already been cleared by Eurofighter. This marks another important step towards multi-role OED with a staggering weapons load on the jet. As predicted, I was airborne after a mere 2,800ft take-off roll in full reheat before I climbed in dry power with 15 degrees nose up to 40,000ft. With six Paveway IIs and six missiles the jet was toting a weapons load equivalent to three legacy platforms. Zooming to 40,000ft in this fit clearly illustrates the impressive nature of the Typhoon's performance and gives an exciting insight into the future of Typhoon operations."

Left: Fast and low, Sqn Ldr Graham Pemberton gets down low over the North Sea during a trial with the OEU. Note the shockwave coming off the canopy generated by the speed and the moist sea air.

Opposite: The twin Eurojet EJ200 jet pipes dominate this rear view of a Typhoon FGR4.

Above: Wg Cdr Toby Craig, Officer Commanding No 17(R) Squadron, leads 'Monkey Flight', a section of Typhoon F2s in the contrails at 35,000ft (10,670m).

Left: 'Typhoon break' – Wg Cdr Toby Craig and Flt Lt Andy Millikin perform a dynamic break for the camera.

Above: As the sun sets at the end of a busy day at No XI(F) Squadron at RAF Coningsby, the Typhoon engineers get busy to prepare the aircraft for the following day's flying.

Right: The fully-loaded swing-role Eurofighter Typhoon FGR4 can tackle aerial threats, drop its precision weapons and then fight its way back out.

AIR DEFENDER

Panavia Tornado F3

The Panavia Tornado F3 is now sharing the air-defence of the UK with Typhoon, but for many years it has been the primary 'AD' fighter of the RAF. Developed from the Tornado IDS as a long-range and high-endurance platform to counter Soviet strategic bombers in the Cold War, the F3 of today is still a very capable fighter aircraft. In recent years the F3 has benefited from a number of incremental upgrades and now carries the fully integrated AIM-120 Advanced Medium Range Air to Air Missile (AMRAAM) and the AIM-132 Advanced Short Range Air to Air Missile (ASRAAM). These capabilities are allied with the impressive Link-16 Joint Tactical Information Distribution System (JTIDS) to give the F3 a potent capability that has attracted much praise despite the plans for it ultimately to be replaced by the Typhoon. The F3 remains operational at RAF Leuchars with famous front-line units Nos 43(F) and 111(F) Squadrons, with No 25(F) Squadron at RAF Leeming planned to draw down operations on the type in March 2008. The aircraft currently used by No 25(F) Squadron will be allocated to 43(F) and 111(F) Squadrons.

Flt Lt Sam Martin is a 1,000 hour F3 instructor pilot at F3 OCU No 56(R) Squadron 'Firebirds' at RAF Leuchars, the last bastion station of F3 operations. "Here at the OCU we train ab initio aircrews and groundcrews and

Above: The F3 is a very powerful twin-engined interceptor. In the words of one pilot: "Nothing else accelerates like an F3, which means we can get where we need to be quickly". The grey nosecone houses the potent AI24 Foxhunter radar now upgraded to Stage 3 standard and better than ever.

Left: The Panavia Tornado F3 was developed from the Tornado IDS as a long-range and high-endurance platform to counter Soviet strategic bombers in the Cold War. The F3 of today is a very capable fighter in the right hands. In this case it is Wg Cdr David Hazell, Officer Commanding No 56(R) Squadron at RAF Leuchars.

Opposite: The Tornado F3 aircrew team consists of the pilot and weapon systems officer (WSO).

also conduct refresher training. We run QWI courses for our weapons specialists, who receive high-end knowledge in our weapons of choice (AMRAAM, ASRAAM) as well as gunnery techniques, and are well versed in tactics against a range of threats including the most modern adversaries we could meet. The F3 is a very powerful twin-engined interceptor and students are expected to learn quickly how to fly the jet to its absolute limit at the very edge of the flight envelope. While we don't necessarily have the performance of the best Russian or US fighter jets, a well-flown F3 is still a force to be reckoned with. The F3 has a powerful and well-integrated radar system and the jet we are flying now is the F3 in its ultimate evolution."

In the words of one F3 pilot: "Nothing else accelerates like an F3, which means we can get where we need to be quickly, which is great for our QRA role". The F3's datalink allows the weapon systems officer (WSO) in the back seat to receive and transmit real time

Above: F3 pilot Flt Lt Sam Martin prepares for another gruelling air combat training mission.

Left: A Tornado F3 accelerates out towards the coast to meet its adversary. In recent years the F3 has benefited from a number of incremental upgrades and now totes the fully integrated AIM-120 Advanced Medium Range Air-to-Air Missile (AMRAAM) and the AIM-132 Advanced Short Range Air-to-Air Missile (ASRAAM). These capabilities are allied to the coveted Link-16 Joint Tactical Information Distribution System (JTIDS) to give the F3 a potent capability that has attracted much praise.

'air pictures' to the airborne mission commander in the E-3 Sentry via datalink. The 2007 upsurge in Russian military aircraft patrols saw the F3s in increased action patrolling UK airspace – protecting the northern approaches of the UK air defence region, a role it was designed for and is ideally suited to. The aircraft has good loiter time and long-range and it can be in-flight refuelled, making it perfect for the interceptor and air defence role. One pilot commented: "Our QRA missions can be asymmetric terrorist threats and this is something we have to consider, but we have been very carefully briefed on all scenarios. We can also respond to the threat from other military aircraft that threaten UK airspace."

Since the end of Operation 'Corporate', the UK has maintained a strong deterrent force in the Falkland Islands. The primary role of the air element of BFFI (British Forces Falkland Islands) is air defence and four Tornado F3s of No 1435 Flight remain there along with a VC10 tanker, a Hercules C-130, and support helicopters. F3 crews are enthusiastic about the Falklands flying due to the lack of airspace restrictions and the fact that the local population is very pleased to see the jets in action, as in the UK, manning a QRA 24-hours a day, 365 days a year.

Right: The F3 is in the twilight of its career but the upgrades it has received mean that the squadrons of today are now flying the F3 in its ultimate evolution. The 'Golden 40' are the fleet of most advanced F3s fully equipped with SIFF (Successor Identification Friend or Foe), upgraded cooling for ops in warmer climates, JTIDS and TRD (Towed Radar Decoy).

Following pages, left: Punching out a heat-seeking missile decoy flare, this F3 is from the 'Firebirds' of No 56(R) Squadron and is seen with its swing-wings fully swept.

Following pages, right: A Tornado F3 soars towards the heavens powered by its twin RB199 Mk104 engines.

STRIKE HARD

Panavia Tornado GR4

Having originally entered front-line service back in 1982 with No IX(B) Squadron as the GR1, the Tornado strike variant (IDS) has performed valiant service and delivered the RAF's punch through three major conflicts. It policed the skies of Iraqi No-Fly zones for 12 years, and now massively upgraded to GR4 standard, provides the RAF's premier attack capability. Its pilot and WSO aircrews, augmented by dedicated tactical support teams, are daily engaged in supporting British troops on the ground in some of the most intensive close air support missions flown for many years. Today's front-line squadron Tornado GR4s are combat veterans with a proven track record over 25 years of service in the demanding theatres that the RAF has operated in around the globe.

Conceived as a low-level strike platform designed to penetrate European Cold War targets, the versatile Tornado has seen extensive action over the harsh deserts of the Middle East, operating at both low and medium levels in a diversity of roles from precision strike to reconnaissance. The current GR4s bristle with the latest technology and an unsurpassed weapon inventory. More capability is on the way in the form of planned upgrades and urgent requirements as the RAF looks to keep these Tornados in service until around 2025, which means that the oldest jets could be over 40 years old when retired.

In the past, the RAF Tornado squadrons were allocated specialist roles, such as No IX(B) Squadron with SEAD (Suppression of Enemy Air Defence), but the flexibility now built into the jet, as well as the training of the aircrew, means that every squadron is able to operate skilfully in all roles. However, each squadron is allocated the lead of a particular capability in order that a specialist understanding is maintained. In terms of new technology, the baseline BAE Systems GR4/4A upgrade has been followed by a series of rolling upgrade 'Packages' to introduce new capabilities for the front-line squadrons, such as the potent

Above and top: The beast's lair – in the depths of the Hardened Aircraft Shelter (HAS) a Tornado GR4 of No 12(B) Squadron comes to life as the pilot and WSO work with the ground crew to start the complex systems and prepare to taxi out for a local training mission.

Left: 'Cobra strike' – a pair of Panavia Tornado GR4s of No XIII Squadron, radio callsign 'Cobra', break for action during a training mission from home station RAF Marham.

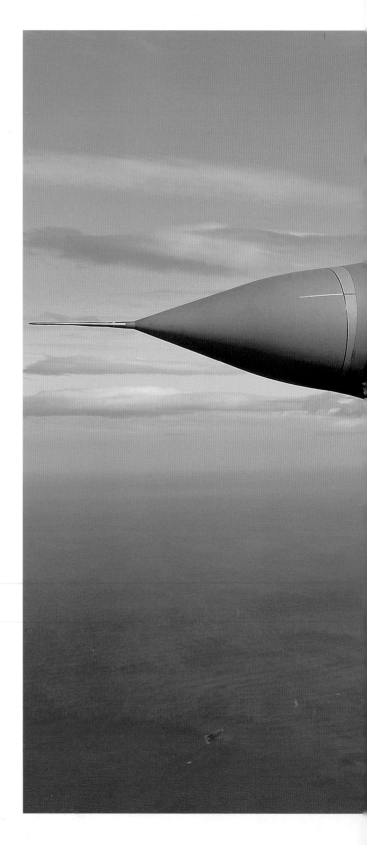

Storm Shadow stand-off weapon and Brimstone anti-armour weaponry. The aircraft's main computer has been further enhanced and the Litening III targeting pod was integrated during 2006.

On A Crusade

The Tornado GR4 force is enjoying a wealth of new capabilities that build on the baseline GR4 upgrade and the type remains in service with both Lossiemouth's No 140 EAW and RAF Marham's No 138 EAW, each with four squadrons. The Marham wing consists of Nos II(AC), IX(B), XIII and 31 Squadrons. RAF Lossiemouth is home to No XV(R) Squadron, the Tornado Operational Conversion Unit, as well as Nos 12(B), 14 and 617 Squadrons. No 14 Squadron 'Crusaders' is led by experienced Tornado WSO Wg Cdr Adrian Frost (known as 'Frosty') and the unit is as active as ever, operating to an incredibly hectic programme with a plethora of operational and training commitments. No 14 Squadron is the lead RAF GR4 unit for targeting pods and precision-guided munitions – a busy task given the reality that these capabilities are key to the nature of current airpower.

Wg Cdr Frost: "As the GR4 Force celebrated 25 years of the Tornado GR in service, the arrival of the Litening III targeting pod, which No 14 Squadron first deployed on operations on 1 February 2007, was heralded as a quantum leap in capability and was excellent news for the force. The capabilities of the pod now mean that we can rapidly achieve PID (Positive Identification) of ground targets and we are able to clearly monitor enemy movements, or the activities of our troops on the ground; we can even live link our cockpit video to them. It is no exaggeration to say that the new pod has transformed our ability to do our job and we have received excellent feedback from the troops we are supporting. Once we have 'slaved' the pod into an urban area, the troops can literally talk our eyes onto a building in seconds. With instant 'eyes on', we can support them as they work their way through built-up areas, monitoring their route ahead, covering the back alleyways, and ready to strike instantly if they need our support. The GR4 will typically remain on station twice as long as other fighters and we have proven extremely relevant and versatile for the current mission in Iraq – a nice reality for a jet in its 25th year of service. We have also looked closely at flying targeting pods in conjunction with our Brimstone anti-armour weapon, which gives added versatility with this smaller and more direct weapon. Recently, on Operation 'Telic' in Iraq, No 617 Squadron was kept particularly busy with the US surge in Baghdad and we regularly support both US and Iraqi forces, flying missions of up to eight hours. The feedback from the troops on the ground has been consistently favourable.

The GR4 is significantly better than it was a few years ago. The Upgraded Main Computer is a modern Pentium-Processor-based system and in conjunction

with a new highly accurate 'blended' navigation mode the versatility of the GR4 has been transformed. Our ability to self-generate precise target co-ordinates with this new capability is particularly significant regarding CAS and targets of opportunity, when possible collateral damage is a particular concern."

At the other end of the experience scale, Fg Off Laurence Chapman, 24, is a WSO on the GR4 Force at No XIII Squadron at Marham. "Following my graduation from the WSO training system I joined the OCU at 'Lossie' before coming to Marham in June 2005. Since then I have deployed to Al Udeid for Operation 'Telic' twice and have mainly flown CAS for ground troops around Baghdad. Our 'show of force' tactic is commonplace to break up trouble and we are accustomed to low-level flying as it is still an important capability for us. The Tornado is an amazing jet and we have a lot going on with the force. Deployment is part of the job for us. In the Gulf our ground crews work solidly with 12 hour shifts to ensure we have the aircraft ready and available. The jets fly a lot of hours out there but you can count on the ground crews to have a full complement of jets available day after day. Our Intelligence Officers have a constant flow of information coming in and they brief us about exactly what is going on in Theatre. Once airborne we are ready for action in whatever role we are tasked for, be it the dead of night or at midday."

Left: A pair of Tornado GR4s of No 14 Squadron at RAF Lossiemouth prepare to dive onto a target on the nearby training ranges at Tain.

Opposite: No II (Army Co-operation) Squadron at RAF Marham is the lead unit for the Raptor (Reconnaissance Airborne Pod for Tornado), illustrated here by a Squadron Tornado GR4A – the reconnaissance-optimised version of the GR4.

Previous pages, left: The picturesque Moray Firth coastline provides a spectacular backdrop to Lossiemouth-based Tornado GR4s.

Previous pages, right: Tornado GR4s of Nos 12(B) and 14 Squadrons, toting Paveway II laser-guided bombs and Brimstone anti-armour weapons respectively. Conceived as a low-level strike platform designed to penetrate European Cold War targets, the versatile Tornado has seen extensive action over the harsh deserts of the Middle East, operating at both low and medium levels in a diversity of roles from precision strike to reconnaissance.

Left: In Operation 'Telic', RAF Tornado GR4s are busy supporting troops on the ground in Iraq. This No IX(B) Squadron GR4 carries a standard 'Theatre' loadout of Enhanced Paveway II (EPW2) precision-guided bomb, Joint Reconnaissance Pod (JRP) and the new Litening III targeting pod.

Photograph by Mike Jorgenson

Opposite: The stunning scenery of the Grampian mountains towards Braemar weathers a distant shower as a Tornado GR4 of No 14 Squadron trains at low level. Tornado GR4 crews are masters of low-level flying, a demanding but very important skill.

Right: At the culmination of a mission, ground crews refuel a Tornado GR4 at Marham. A front-line fast-jet squadron comprises of around 120 ground crew, 40 aircrew and a diversity of support staff including intelligence and administration officers – all contributing to a big team effort.

ON TIME, ON TARGET

Strike Training With No XIII Squadron

It is 0630hrs on a crisp autumn morning at RAF Marham in Norfolk. Already, No XIII Tornado GR4 Squadron is a hive of activity. The Squadron Intelligence Officer has been putting the final touches to a briefing for the squadron commander, Wg Cdr Terry Jones, regarding an Air Tasking Order that the Unit has received from operations. It involves two of the Squadron's Tornado GR4s being called in to strike a target with retarded 1,000lb 'dumb' bombs. The target is well to the north and needs to be struck by the jets from ultra-low level with pinpoint timing. The Squadron's expert armourers have been working hard since the night before to get the weapons ready and loaded onto the jets and the maintenance crews have been putting in the hours as ever to make sure the aircraft are ready and in peak serviceability. On regular occasions for the RAF this is a real combat mission. However, today this is standard (but crucial) training, vital day-to-day practice for a front-line squadron to ensure it is ready to meet its next combat role, whatever it may be. With the mission planned by the WSOs, target runs plotted on the Tornado Mission Planner (TAMPA), briefings complete, the crews for 'Cobra Flight' outbrief and 'walk' to the awaiting GR4s.

Having been seen out by the dedicated line crews, the Tornados taxi out to the main runway at Marham, under the guidance of the Air Traffic Controllers in the tower. "Cobra, you are clear take-off", comes the call and the Tornados roar to full afterburner and accelerate off. Within minutes they are cruising up the east coast towards the training range, with the crews taking the time to run through pre-strike checks and preparing to let down for a low-level ingress to their remote target, the Cape Wrath Range on the northernmost tip of Scotland. Descending into low level, the jets dip below the hills, charge past rocky outcrops, pull hard to make the next turning point and dive for the sanctuary of the next valley. The pilots in the Tornado GR4s are working hard to stay low as they tear across the remote Scottish

countryside at a minimum level of 250ft (75m), working the systems in the jet, staying low, making split-second timings on the route. This kind of low-level flying training is vitally important for the RAF pilots to ensure they stay sharp in this harshest of environments.

"Cape Wrath Range, this is Cobra Flight." As the weather closes in, the Tornado crews use their advanced avionics and terrain-following radar (TFR) to hug the contours and then head out over the sea, skimming the waves, heading for the target. The first of four 'hot' passes follows and crews drop the concrete-filled practice bombs with total precision on the remote crag of rock that is used as a bombing target. On time, and on target – mission accomplished!

Wg Cdr Terry Jones is Officer Commanding No XIII Squadron. "Being a Tornado GR4 squadron commander is very hard work and a constant challenge, but a huge honour. Our manpower was reduced recently and we have had to look at the way we work to become more

efficient to maintain our output level; I am pleased to say we have achieved that. On the Squadron we have in the order of 120 ground crew, 40 aircrew and a diversity of support staff including intelligence officers, administration officers, safety equipment fitters – it is a big team effort. We are currently going on combat operations every 14 months and in between we have to try to match our training to all the scenarios that may come up – from the extremely difficult high-intensity conflict missions through to our inevitable Gulf-type

Above: Tornado Team – Wg Cdr Terry Jones, Officer Commanding No XIII Squadron, flanked by Sqn Ldr Gordon Melville and Fg Off Jen Shackley.

Opposite: 'Cobra Flight' – having departed RAF Marham, Sqn Ldr Gordon Melville and Fg Off Jen Shackley transit at 20,000ft (6,100m) towards the training area in their Tornado GR4.

roles. I have to ensure we are achieving the right balance in the training and making sure we have capable people and good equipment that work together as a well-oiled machine. The quality of our training in the UK is constantly improving and now our debriefing facilities here are second to none – they are the same quality that was previously unique to an exercise such as Red Flag in the USA. People joining the RAF now get to do what they train to do. We get to put all our training into action."

The RAF is continually evolving to support its assets, such as the Tornado GR4 Force, in the smartest and most cost-effective way to make the most of increasingly stretched budgets. The RAF has sought to streamline the process of maintenance and has introduced rolling technology upgrade insertions for the type. The Combined Maintenance and Upgrade facility now established at RAF Marham is being run jointly by BAE Systems and the RAF in a partnering arrangement to allow upgrades to be embodied more efficiently during routine maintenance. For a country that takes such a proactive stance on the world stage it is important to ensure that the men and women on the front line continue to get the best possible tools to do the job. The amazing work of our armed forces in difficult operating theatres is daily news. Airpower is vital in supporting these ground forces through CAS, and this is a particular role where the Tornado GR4 is now excelling.

Above: Armed with concrete-filled retarded 1,000lb bombs and live cannon rounds as well as 250litre drop tanks and Sky Shadow electronic countermeasure pods, two No XIII Squadron Tornado GR4s show off their impressive arsenals.

Left: The Tornado GR4 can sweep its wings back to 45 and 67 degrees. Here, Sqn Ldr Gordon Melville accelerates with wings right back at 67 degrees and shows off the two 1,000lb bombs that the GR4 is clutching to its belly.

Opposite: With twin RB199 engines in full reheat a Tornado GR4 prepares for take-off.

Following pages: Sweeping in over the coast at Dunbar – the two Marham-based Tornado GR4s of No XIII Squadron get down low to avoid the prying eyes of potential adversaries. The GR4 is extremely capable at low level and is able to get low and fast to escape enemy fighters if engaged.

Opposite: Turning in towards the live bombing range on Garvie Island on the remote northern tip of Scotland.

Right: "Three, two, one… bomb gone!"

Below: Having dropped their weapons, the Marham-based Tornado GR4s fuel-stop at Lossiemouth, where the Visiting Aircraft Section (VAS) offer a sterling support service.

Above: The Tornado GR4 can be called into action around the clock. The jet's advanced avionics represent the latest technology, supporting an unsurpassed weapon inventory.

Right: Mission accomplished – 'Cobra Flight' head back to Marham at the culmination of a very successful day's training.

CLOSE AIR SUPPORT

BAE Systems Harrier GR9

The Harrier is one of the most unmistakable of RAF types. The Harrier II in service today, which is vastly different to its original incarnation, fulfils a vital role for the UK armed forces and is set to do so well into the next decade when it will be replaced by the F-35 Joint Combat Aircraft. Joint Force Harrier (JFH) is currently transitioning to an all Harrier GR9 and T12 trainer fleet operated by No 122 EAW, comprised of Nos 1(F) and IV(AC) Squadrons and the Naval Strike Wing (NSW) at RAF Cottesmore, and the OCU, No 20(R) Squadron, at the nearby 'spiritual home of the Harrier' at RAF Wittering.

In recent times the Harrier Force has been operating to a busy pace supporting Operation 'Herrick' in Afghanistan, with any one of the squadrons deployed at any given time. Officer Commanding No 1(F) Squadron in 2007 was Wg Cdr Andy Lewis. "Joint Force Harrier has been deployed to Kandahar Airfield in support of NATO (including British) and Coalition ground forces since 2004. During that time the Force has provided extensive reconnaissance and CAS to friendly ground forces engaged with hostile elements. Our tasks have ranged from providing a 'presence' over the battlefield to delivering precision-guided munitions against targets engaged at close quarters with our own forces. The Harrier has performed superbly and demonstrated its flexibility time and again both in operating from a bare base airfield, thousands of miles from home, and in the range of weaponry it brings to the fight at short notice." Today's Harrier Force is very much a joint approach to operations, having subsumed personnel from the Royal Navy Sea Harrier community. The joint approach to operations is clearly illustrated here with the men and women working alongside each other at RAF

Right: The unmistakable lines of the BAE Systems Harrier GR9 of Joint Force Harrier from RAF Cottesmore. The nose features the Angle Rate Bombing Set (ARBS), the Forward Looking Infra-Red (FLIR) sensor and the Zeus electronic countermeasures system.

Cottesmore. Lt Cdr Kris Ward is a JFH pilot with the NSW here. "The NSW is commanded by Cdr Kev Seymour and it comprises 800 and 801 Naval Air Squadrons operating as an integrated team alongside Nos 1(F) Squadron and IV(AC) Squadron. Across the board this is a joint approach to operations – with RAF and Naval personnel working together. I am currently preparing to deploy with NSW to support Operation 'Herrick' in Afghanistan for our four-month rotational deployment. At the moment we are getting back up to speed to make sure we are fully capable for all the roles we will undertake out there." Clearly, Operation 'Herrick' is the main driver for the Harrier Force in the RAF's 90th year and at Kandahar the Harriers sit on 24-hour alert, fragged (tasked) to fly sorties as allocated by the CAOC (Combined Air Operations Centre). Another pilot commented, "The Harriers provide 24-hour CAS air cover for Coalition troops on the ground: this has recently been mainly British troops in Helmand Province. Being able to provide air support for the guys on the ground by pinpoint air strikes or just by our mere presence to deter the enemy is fantastic, especially when the troops come back to see us and are able to thank us for literally stepping in to help them out in tight situations."

Major Phil Kelly is executive officer at No 1(F) Squadron and is a further illustration of the joint force approach to Harrier operations as he is a Royal Marine pilot. "I originally joined No 1(F) Squadron as JP (Junior Pilot) and then became a flight commander. I have done three tours in Afghanistan with the Squadron and our operational tempo out there is directly related to the land operation, so when they step up their missions we respond. We get our young squadron personnel to cut their teeth very early now and the quality of the people we have is improving all the time because within a few weeks of leaving the OCU and becoming combat ready they are on operations with live weapons supporting troops in contact with the enemy. It is the best possible grounding for any pilot as you realise the operational imperative. The young guys want to be deployed away, gaining this valuable experience as

often as possible. This is a hugely rewarding time for the Harrier force as it has allowed us to upgrade the jet and make us more combat effective. The IPTs (Integrated Project Teams) have done very well getting the new Sniper targeting pod into service so quickly and it's making a huge difference operationally."

The Lockheed Martin Sniper targeting pod is the latest piece of equipment being rolled out for the Harrier force and it is proving extremely popular and effective. Information from this highly capable new pod can be downloaded to troops on the ground via a real-time feed on a laptop via the Rover downlink. Petty Officer Brian Beyer is an armourer on JFH. "I came here from the Sea Harrier at Yeovilton and have done three tours in Afghanistan. We have been extremely busy on detachment reloading the jets and are using all the weapons in the inventory including CRV-7 rockets, Paveway and Enhanced Paveway precision bombs. Sniper has made life a lot easier for us armourers as we no longer have to remove the pod from the jet for servicing. It is a big improvement and the imagery we get from it is amazing."

Above: The Harrier Force has been operating to a busy pace supporting Operation 'Herrick' in Afghanistan, with any one of the squadrons deployed at any given time. Tasks have ranged from providing a 'presence' over the battlefield to delivering precision-guided munitions against targets engaged at close quarters with our own forces. The Harrier nearest the camera carries mission markings from its deployment to 'Herrick'.

Opposite: This Harrier GR9 is seen carrying the latest equipment for the type. Under the outer wing pylon is the advanced Raytheon Paveway IV precision-guided bomb and the Lockheed Martin Sniper advanced targeting pod is fitted under the fuselage.

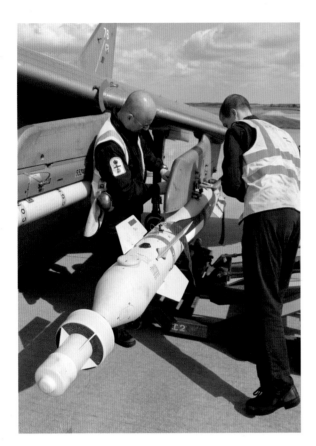

Above: The Harrier is one of the most prized postings in the RAF for pilots. The aircraft is extremely challenging, given its short take-off vertical landing (STOVL) capabilities. This makes it an extremely versatile platform for the RAF.

Above left: Joint Force Harrier armourers load a Raytheon Paveway IV precision-guided bomb on a Harrier GR9.

REBELS WITH A CAUSE

41(R) Squadron

No 41(R) Squadron, the Fast Jet Weapons Operational Evaluation Unit (FJWOEU), is based at RAF Coningsby and is commanded by Wg Cdr Andy Myers. The Squadron (with its well-known radio callsign 'Rebel') is part of the RAF's AWC and is responsible for evaluating the latest technology planned for the front-line Tornado F3 and GR4 and Harrier GR9s. The aim of establishing the FJWOEU in 2004 was to bring fast-jet and weapons operational evaluation together to explore the synergies available to all the platforms, particularly with the co-location of the Typhoon OEU at Coningsby. The Unit can task share and assist with trials work and cross-fertilise and spread information between aircraft platforms as a centre of excellence for fast-jet operational test and evaluation.

Ongoing trials programmes at the Unit reflect the cutting edge of technologies being readied for release to the operational squadrons. In particular, the Harrier GR9 and Tornado GR4 teams at 41(R) Squadron are working intensely to support the operational requirements of units deployed for ongoing combat operations in Afghanistan and Iraq. The widely publicised integration of latest technology targeting pods for these two types is clearly of huge significance for the OEU and the skill and dedication of its personnel has ensured that these latest capabilities are being made available to the front line as soon as possible.

Above: A No IV(AC) Squadron Harrier GR9 darts amongst the valleys of North Wales during a training mission from RAF Cottesmore.

Left: No 1(F) Squadron has operated the Harrier since 1969 when it converted to the Harrier GR1 and became the first operational squadron in the world to fly this unique vertical/short take-off and landing aircraft. Since then the Unit has served in Belize, the South Atlantic during the Falklands Conflict in 1982, and in Afghanistan for Operation 'Herrick'. This Harrier GR7 from the Squadron is seen taking on fuel from an RAF VC10 K3 of No 101 Squadron.

Future Harrier

With Operation 'Herrick' making big demands on the Harriers, training new personnel is a valuable link in the chain to ensure capability is maintained. The OCU at RAF Wittering is working hard to deliver new pilots and groundcrews for JFH. It is also adapting and updating the syllabus to encompass the new capabilities of the upgraded GR9 variant. The squadrons are also tasked with maintaining the deployed capability aboard the UK's aircraft carriers and are now looking ahead to the future and the introduction of the Navy's two new 'Super Carriers' and the F-35 advanced fighter.

The Harrier GR9 avionics upgrade involves 62 aircraft being upgraded from GR7 to GR9 standard, from which the official active inventory of 48 aircraft is drawn. The BAE Systems upgrade includes the introduction of a new mission computer with a MIL-STD-1760 compatible stores management system,

a new head-down display with a video map generator, Ground Proximity Warning System (GPWS), GPS and a new Inertial Navigation System. The new stores management system will enable the aircraft to communicate with new 'smart' weapons such as the Raytheon Paveway IV. The upgrade programme improves the GR9 in four phases: Capability A with a MIL-STD-1760 mission computer, GPS inertial navigation and new stores management systems; Capability B introduces all new avionics systems up to full working specification; Capability C includes the introduction of the first of the new 'smart' weapons for the GR9, the Raytheon Paveway IV 500lb bomb; Capability D includes the Brimstone anti-armour missile planned for introduction during 2008. The GR9 upgrade followed the re-engining of 30 Harriers with the uprated Rolls-Royce Pegasus Mk107 engine to allow the Harrier to operate in hotter climates with greater weapons loads, under the designation GR9A.

On A Mission – Harrier Style

The training briefing by the flight commander starts with an overview. "The mission today revolves around a realistic and complex scenario devised by the Squadron Intelligence Officer (Squinto) and involves us heading up the east coast towards Berwick-Upon-Tweed to locate and 'attack' a primary time-sensitive target of a train that is believed to be carrying chemical weapons."

The Harrier pilots need to find and destroy the train by working closely with the airborne controllers in the E-3D AWACS, who provide a constant update on the battle picture. They also need to keep a keen eye out for marauding 'MiG-29' enemy fighter aircraft and surface to air missiles (SAMs). Of course, this is training, the Harriers will only simulate attacking the train, the marauding MiGs are actually RAF Tornado F3s and the SAMs are only threat rings that need to be accounted for during attack planning. But make no mistake, this is a realistic situation and the pilots are dealing with every element with the utmost professionalism and realism. At the outbrief, a late piece of intelligence is passed to the pilots. HUMINT (Human Intelligence) has reported that some people boarding the train were reported to be carrying 'poles' that could be shoulder-launched anti-aircraft missiles – yet more information to add to the already intense plan. It is this realistic training that keeps RAF and RN personnel at the leading edge of capability, and coupled with the right technology means that when called upon they can do the job required of them.

FORCE PROTECTION

RAF Regiment

In August 1990 when Iraq invaded Kuwait, the RAF undertook its largest deployment since the Falklands Conflict. The RAF Regiment deployed to Cyprus, Bahrain and Saudi Arabia to carry out a variety of duties, including short-range air defence (SHORAD) with the Rapier, NBC (Nuclear, Biological and Chemical) monitoring, ground defence and other specialist tasks. In total, they comprised 19 per cent of the RAF deployed force. The rapid arrival of this force, together with those of other Coalition air forces, acted as a strong deterrent to any aggressive Iraqi move against Saudi Arabia.

Force Protection is the military term given to a range of measures designed to preserve the combat power of our own forces. Aircraft, personnel and facilities and equipment necessary to maintain and operate them are particularly vulnerable to attack on the ground. The RAF discovered this to its cost during the Battle of Crete in 1941, when German airborne forces quickly overran lightly defended airfields. The realisation that air assets required their own robust defences led to the formation of the RAF Regiment in 1942.

Today, the RAF Regiment takes the lead on Force Protection (FP) for the RAF on all operations, including in Afghanistan and Iraq. Regiment squadrons are trained and equipped to prevent a successful enemy attack in the first instance; minimise the damage caused by a successful attack; and ensure that air operations can continue without delay in the aftermath of an attack. The Regiment is an expert body in CBRN (Chemical, Biological, Radiological and Nuclear) defence and is equipped with advanced vehicles and detection measures. When they are not deployed on operations, the Regular and Auxiliary Squadrons of the RAF Regiment and the Operational Support Squadrons of the Royal Auxiliary Air Force, which are distributed across a variety of RAF stations throughout the UK, are grouped under the RAF Regiment Force Protection Wing HQ based at RAF Honington.

Above: Protecting deployed assets is a key role for the RAF Regiment. *Photograph: Crown Copyright*

Opposite above: UK training missions revolve around realistic and complex scenarios designed to best prepare squadrons for deployments to operational theatres.

Right: Vigo Wood at RAF Wittering provides an ideal training facility for Harrier pilots to practise operating in confined spaces. The home-stationed No 20(R) Squadron, the Harrier OCU, can also make use of a take-off ramp that is installed here to help prepare pilots to embark on the Royal Navy aircraft carriers, another vital element that makes the Harrier an extremely deployable asset.

Opposite: The Harrier GR9 upgrade and associated improvements will keep RAF Harriers viable until replaced by the Lockheed Martin F-35 Joint Combat Aircraft (JCA).

Above: Flt Lt Ben Shepard prepares for a night training mission from RAF Cottesmore. A pilot's night combat-ready clearance involves use of the Harrier's Forward Looking Infra-Red (FLIR) sensor and Night Vision Goggles (NVGs).

Right: Night attack puts the Harrier GR9 in its element. The night-attack variant of the Harrier II was developed from 1984 and was designated the GR7 by the RAF, with deliveries from 1989. Deliveries consisted of converted GR5 variants and new production examples – all of which were completed by 1995.

ELECTRONIC WARRIORS
Intelligence, Surveillance, Target Acquisition and Reconnaissance

RAF Waddington sits within sight of the impressive Lincoln Cathedral. This is an area rich in RAF history and tradition, so it is highly apt that it is this Station that is breaking new ground for the Service. The arrival of the ASTOR-equipped (Airborne STand-Off Radar) Bombardier Sentinel R1 with No 5(AC) Squadron at Waddington to operate alongside the resident E-3D Sentrys and Nimrod R1s has cemented the reputation of Waddington as the RAF's ISTAR (Intelligence, Surveillance, Target Acquisition and Reconnaissance) hub. The resident No 34 Expeditionary Air Wing (EAW) represents the cutting edge of RAF technology as it moves into an era of networked battlefield capabilities.

EYES IN THE SKIES

Boeing E-3D Sentry

The Boeing E-3D Sentry AEW1 forms the heart of this ISTAR capability, a linchpin in the overall capability for the RAF. Having entered service in 1990 as a replacement for the ageing Avro Shackleton, the seven E-3Ds represent the UK component of the NATO Airborne Early Warning (AEW) Force. More importantly, they represent a networked capability that absorbs electronic information from other platforms to meld and build an overall picture of the modern battlespace. In front-line service with Nos 8 and 23 Squadrons at Waddington, the aircraft provide airborne early warning and control services to both UK and NATO air defence forces. They work closely with air defence agencies to form a strong team able to collect, analyse and relay vital information to key nodes.

Squadron Leader Tim Brown is a Fighter Controller by trade and is an instructor at No 54(R) Squadron at Waddington, a unit that is now known as the ISTAR OCU. "The E-3D typically flies with 11 mission crewmembers in the back in addition to the three airborne technicians and four flight deck crew. The Weapons Team is directly responsible for directing the battle under the Tactical Director, who is the overall mission commander.

Previous pages, left: The badges of No 54(R) Squadron and the NATO Airborne Early Warning Force (NAEWF) adorn the nose of this E-3D Sentry at Waddington.

Previous pages, right: Waddington's ISTAR 'Triad' – a Boeing E-3D Sentry leads a Nimrod R1 of No 51 Squadron and a Sentinel R1 of No 5(AC) Squadron. Waddington's No 34 Expeditionary Air Wing (EAW) is the RAF's highly advanced ISTAR (Intelligence, Surveillance, Target Acquisition and Reconnaissance) hub. *Photograph by Geoffrey H. Lee*

Above: On patrol – the rotordome that houses the potent AN/APY-2 radar is shown to good effect as an E-3D cruises at altitude during a UK air defence mission. The aircraft's advanced sensors collect and assimilate data to build a Recognised Air and Surface Picture (RASP) of the area it is operating in.

Photograph by Geoffrey H. Lee

The majority of us down the back of the E-3 are junior officers and senior NCOs, with trades varying from fighter controller to weapon systems operator (WSOp), so there's a real mix of experience and backgrounds that helps make us such a strong team. I act as a fighter allocator and supervisor of the weapons team and we are basically tasked with looking at activity in the airspace as well as the surface picture (sea or ground). The surveillance operators have assigned blocks of airspace and they identify and classify contacts that we pick up via our sensors, be it by our AN/APY-2 radar in the rotordome, the Identification Friend or Foe (IFF), or the Electronic Support Measures (ESM) systems. By collecting and assimilating this data we build a Recognised Air and Surface Picture (RASP) that we can use to build situational awareness and then task the 'packages' of aircraft we are controlling, which can be bombers, fighters going to intercept, or in-flight refuelling assets that are supporting the overall operation.

As a fighter controller we are sometimes known as the 'third voice in the cockpit'. We are looking at the big picture out there. Our radar has far greater range than a fighter radar, we are a big platform and we are carrying more power and weight than a fighter and so we are able to scan a far bigger portion of airspace. We also have an additional element we can use to build the big picture. Through Link-16/JTIDS (Joint Tactical Information Distribution System) we can datalink with fighters and other assets to 'look' into all areas of interest. This means that a fighter could upload datalink information to us, for instance a low-level contact in his area we can't see because it is down low in a valley – despite our capabilities no radars can look through terrain. The fighter can back-link the information to us, enabling us to further build the RASP."

An E-3D is, of course, only potent when it is in the air. As with all RAF squadrons, keeping the assets flying is as important as the airborne mission itself. Flt Lt Simon Middleditch is one of three Junior Engineering Officers (JEngOs) at the Sentry Maintenance Squadron at Waddington. "As JEngO I am responsible for the

seven E-3Ds and I have to ensure that we can meet the flying programme for the three squadrons here that are operating the type. I am in charge of one of two shifts of approximately 90 people working long days and nights. As the link between the aircrew and groundcrew, I try to get out of the office as often as possible and talk to our teams as I feel good communication plays a major part in our success.

On the E-3D we effectively have six trade areas: propulsion, airframes, mission system radar, mission system computer, air vehicle communications/electrical and air vehicle avionics. As part of modernisation, these have now been restructured to two base levels of mechanical and avionics. The newcomers to RAF technical trades go through basic

recruit training at RAF Halton before heading off to mechanical training at DCAE Cosford. They then emerge as Aircraft Maintenance Mechanics and will come to a squadron with a bias towards avionics or mechanical trades. After two years or so they will return to Cosford for lengthy further technical training. My job is to employ these technicians to their full potential and keep the aircrew happy. I have a very diverse role with lots of challenges – it's fantastic and I love doing it."

Above: The RAF operates seven E-3D Sentry AEW (Airborne Early Warning) aircraft, each charismatically named after the 'Seven Dwarfs' from Walt Disney's classic animated movie *Snow White and the Seven Dwarfs*.

SECRET MISSIONS

Nimrod R1

Without question one of the RAF's most clandestine operations is run by No 51 Squadron at Waddington – a true intelligence-gathering unit. The Squadron can trace its current mission back to 1958 when it began operations as a Special Duties squadron in Signals Command flying de Havilland Comets and a variety of Canberras on surveillance flights from RAF Wyton. In 1974 the Comets were replaced by a specialised version of the Nimrod, the R1. The mission of the Squadron's three highly tasked Nimrod R1s is ELINT (electronics intelligence) and COMINT (communications intelligence). This basically equates to the ability to locate and analyse radar emissions and communications traffic. The crews that fly the Nimrods and those that support them on the ground are some of the most highly experienced and skilled found anywhere in the RAF.

Identified by the lack of a rear-mounted MAD (Magnetic Anomaly Detector) 'sting tail', the three original Nimrod R1s were procured in the late 1960s to fulfil the RAF's strategic signals intelligence (SIGINT) requirement. They were subsequently equipped with a highly-classified suite of reconnaissance and electronic intelligence-gathering equipment installed by the RAF.

Above: The Nimrod R1s of No 51 Squadron conduct highly classified missions collecting valuable Electronic and Communications Intelligence.

EYES ABOVE THE BATTLEFIELD

Sentinel R1

Completing the ISTAR 'Triad' at Waddington is the newest arrival at the Station – the brand new Sentinel R1 ASTOR. Sentinel represents an airborne surveillance platform with unparalleled capability, producing a detailed real-time radar picture of the battlespace which force commanders can use to study the movement and disposition of friendly and enemy forces on the ground.

Operated by No 5(AC) Squadron, which reformed here on 1 April 2004 under the command of Wg Cdr Bill Hughes, this highly sophisticated Intelligence, Surveillance and Reconnaissance platform is being developed by Raytheon Systems Limited, based on the Bombardier Global Express business jet airframe. The five highly modified RAF aircraft provide a sophisticated ground surveillance capability, thanks to the incorporation of an enhanced version of the Raytheon ASARS-2 Synthetic Aperture/Moving Target Indication (SAR/MTI) radar. This system generates high-resolution images of the terrain and static targets, while the MTI tracks ground targets on the move – a vital tool for monitoring the battlefield. Much like the USAF Northrop Grumman E-8 JSTARS, the RAF's ASTOR is able to track, exploit and datalink information to commanders or other platforms in near real-time. Since the Squadron stood up in 2004, it has been working hard to develop this new and unique capability, working towards Full Operating Capability status in 2009.

The requirement for this type of battlefield surveillance dates back to the Cold War when the Corps Airborne Stand-Off Radar (CASTOR) programme led to a specially modified B-N Islander being used as a

Left: The first RAF Sentinel R1 ZJ690 was flown from the Bombardier factory in Canada to Raytheon's facility at Greenville, Texas, on 31 January 2002, where the aircraft underwent conversion and equipment installation. This aircraft flew for the first time in full Sentinel R1 configuration on 26 May 2004. *Photograph by Geoffrey H. Lee*

demonstrator for a Moving Target Indicator (MTI) radar to enable tracking and identification of troop concentrations or convoy movements. This led to the joint RAF/Army ASTOR programme we see in service today.

The most notable modification to the Global Express airframe is the large 15ft (4.6m) canoe fairing under the fuselage that houses the dual-mode Raytheon radar. On top of the fuselage is a large satellite communications (SATCOMs) radome, a key feature for an aircraft designed to glean information and transmit its radar imagery to the ground for exploitation, or to be analysed on board with the aircraft operating autonomously. The wealth of gathered information can be stored for post-flight analysis and interpretation, or it can be datalinked in near real-time to ground stations using its Wideband DataLink Subsystem (WDLS). As well as feeding data to the dedicated ASTOR ground stations, the radar imagery can be passed directly to other airborne ISTAR platforms such as the E-3D. With Waddington as the ISTAR hub, there is clearly huge potential for the three home-based platforms to meld information through a combination of datalinks or voice links and build 'the bigger picture'. In the words of one RAF officer, "It's a veritable feast of information out there".

Training the TRIAD

No 54(R) Squadron at Waddington is responsible for training all E-3D aircrews as well as the mission crews for the Nimrod R1 – with Sentinel training also set to be established here. The ex-Jaguar unit was formed from elements of No 23 Squadron's Sentry Training Flight, the No 51 Squadron Training Flight and from elements of the Waddington Mission Support Wing and Mission Simulator Flight, borrowing aircraft from the front-line as required.

Right: An underfuselage fairing accommodates the Raytheon ASARS-2 Synthetic Aperture/Moving Target Indication (SAR/MTI) radar on the Sentinel R1. The system generates images of the terrain while the MTI can track ground targets on the move.

Photograph by Geoffrey H. Lee

Left: The Sentinel R1s operated by No 5(AC) Squadron represent an airborne surveillance platform with unparalleled capability, producing a detailed real-time radar picture of the battlespace which force commanders can use to study the movement and disposition of friendly and enemy forces on the ground.

Below: Modifications to the basic Global Express airframe include the large 15ft (4.6m) canoe fairing under the fuselage that houses the dual-mode Raytheon radar and a large satellite communications (SATCOMs) radome on top of the fuselage.

Photograph Geoffrey H. Lee

Above: No 39 Squadron consists of pilots, sensor operators, engineers and other support personnel. The pilots and sensor operators work round-the-clock at Ground Control Stations at Nellis AFB, to provide vital services such as close air support (CAS), surveillance and air strike co-ordination. This image shows a sensor operator at work controlling the Predator's suite of advanced avionics. *Photograph: Crown Copyright*

Above right: Since 2004 the RAF has been engaged in joint General Atomics RQ-1 Predator UAV operations with the USAF. Here, RAF technicians inspect a Predator after a mission. *Photograph: Crown Copyright*

SILENT WARRIORS

Unmanned Aerial Vehicles

The RAF continually strives to stay at the leading edge of new technology as it emerges. Unmanned Aerial Vehicles (UAVs) have become a vital element of modern air power operations, with the US leading the way with platforms such as the General Atomics RQ-1 Predator-A. Under an Urgent Operational Requirement raised in 2004, the RAF formally allied itself with joint RQ-1 operations alongside the USAF and established No 1115 Flight to operate in close co-operation with USAF units at Creech AFB, Nevada. Now officially re-formed as No 39 Squadron, this unique unit is parented by RAF Waddington and in late 2007 was preparing to start operations with the latest-generation combat UAV (UCAV) – the MQ-9 Reaper. These UCAVs offer versatile sensor and strike capabilities and will become a vital part of the ISTAR force, with a persistent capability to

execute missions in excess of 24 hours. No 39 Squadron consists of 45 predominantly RAF personnel, comprising pilots, sensor operators, engineers and other support staff. The pilots and sensor operators work round-the-clock at Ground Control Stations housed at Nellis AFB, Nevada, whilst the engineers are based at Creech AFB. Flying the Predator Unmanned Aerial System, they provide vital persistent, wide-area surveillance to support troops on the ground in both Iraq and Afghanistan. If called upon, they can also provide close air support, video support of surface actions, air strike co-ordination and direct fire support.

Looking further into the future, Taranis is a new British UCAV demonstrator programme being developed as part of the UK's Strategic Unmanned Air Vehicle (Experimental) programme (SUAV(E)). Led by BAE Systems, Taranis will result in a UCAV demonstrator with fully integrated autonomous systems and low observable features.

THE MIGHTY HUNTER

Nimrod MR2

Long known as the 'Mighty Hunter', completing the RAF ISTAR picture is its oldest partner – the Nimrod MR2. The Nimrod was developed to replace the Shackleton maritime reconnaissance aircraft and design work under the Hawker Siddeley 801 programme began in June 1964, with the type entering service in 1969. Based substantially upon the airframe of the de Havilland Comet 4C, the Nimrod was designed to combine the advantages of high-altitude, fast-transit speed with low wing loading and good low-speed manoeuvring capabilities when operating in its primary roles of anti-submarine warfare, anti-surface warfare and sea surveillance.

Now centralised with No 325 Expeditionary Air Wing (EAW) at RAF Kinloss, Moray, the 15-strong Nimrod force plays a vital role within the overall armed forces capability. Tasked with anti-submarine and anti-surface warfare, search and rescue, and general surveillance and monitoring duties of the sea around the UK, the Nimrod force has also turned its hand to overland surveillance and this role has increased steadily over recent years as the need for Time Sensitive Targeting has been realised. The versatility of the Nimrod and its crews has resulted in a host of new developments and concepts of use for the aircraft, including electro-optical IMINT (Image Intelligence) surveillance and communications support to coalition ground troops deployed in operational theatres.

The Nimrod MR2 community has turned its hand to reacting to emerging combat requirements, reflecting the RAF ethos of adaptability and eagerness to support operations. Wg Cdr Iain Torrance is a seasoned Nimrod pilot, "We have retained our traditional maritime roles, be it in the anti-submarine or anti-surface warfare role. We also retain our more traditional support roles for fishery protection, search and rescue and surveillance of the coastline, which as a maritime nation remains highly important for us. However, we have been quick to adapt to support ground forces. This is a relatively new environment for us that has developed over the last five years, but it comes in addition to our more traditional roles."

At Kinloss, Nos 120 and 201 Squadrons form the Nimrod front line, alongside No 42(R) Squadron, the OCU. A typical Nimrod mission crew comprises 12-13 personnel based on two pilots, an air engineer, three WSOs (two navigators and an air electronics officer), two acoustics operators and four dry sensor operators – although this can be tailored as dictated by a particular mission. The type's new MX-15 electro-optical (EO) sensor has transformed the Nimrod's ability to perform overland support missions. Wg Cdr Torrance: "We are involved in Operations 'Herrick' and 'Telic', where we have detachments giving situational awareness to ground forces, which is valuable to their own self protection, but also proves just as valuable when they are on the offensive. We are using our EO kit to pass information to them they would not be able to get themselves." It is clear that there has been a considerable amount of pressure on the Nimrod fleet as it has responded to additional taskings, which can only reflect very positively on the attitudes of both the groundcrew and aircrew, who are continuously deploying around the world.

Below: When required, two of the Nimrod's four Spey engines can be shut down to extend endurance when they are on task. The aircraft can also climb and cruise on only one engine in emergency situations. *Photograph by Derek Bower*

Above and right: The in-flight refuelling probe is shown to good effect in these images. The ability to refuel in-flight allows the Nimrod to stay on station for many hours, a valuable asset when called upon to support troops on the ground.

Left: The Nimrod is based on the de Havilland Comet 4C, designed to combine the advantages of high-altitude, fast-transit speed with low wing loading and good low-speed manoeuvring capabilities. This example is seen returning from the 'Neptune Warrior' maritime exercise held from its home station RAF Kinloss. *Photograph by Richard Cooper*

Below: No 325 Expeditionary Air Wing (EAW) at RAF Kinloss, Moray, operates the RAF Nimrod MR2 force and fulfils requirements in the anti-submarine and anti-surface warfare, search and rescue, and maritime surveillance roles, as well as overland surveillance. The versatility of the Nimrod and its crews has resulted in a range of new roles for the force.

Future Nimrod

As testament to the longevity and suitability of the Nimrod airframe, BAE Systems is breathing new life into the aircraft and producing to all intents and purposes what is a completely new aircraft – the Nimrod MRA4. The Return-To-Works (RTW) programme is much more than a mid-life upgrade, and will provide a zero-houred new fleet of aircraft for the RAF with the latest capabilities. As with the majority of ambitious aviation programmes, MRA4 has suffered from delays. However, ever since the first example, ZJ516, made its maiden flight from BAE Systems Woodford on 26 August 2004, the programme has started showing its true potential.

The airframes are completely rebuilt and refitted with Rolls-Royce BR710 engines and the new Searchwater 2000MR surveillance radar. The planned 12 MRA4s will have a full suite of datalinks and the community at Kinloss is eagerly awaiting the arrival of the aircraft as they are rolled out by BAE Systems. Wg Cdr Torrance said of the MRA4. "To take what we do today onto a new platform with new capabilities will be a challenge for us. The new aircraft will operate fundamentally differently to what we have now; the amount and quantity of information we will absorb and be able to disseminate will be hugely different. We plan to scale down MR2 operations as the MRA4 ramps up, with the first training course planned to start here at the end of 2009. The course will be developed in part by BAE Warton and Kinloss to train our instructors at No 42(R) Squadron. Initial Operating Capability will be marked by five aircraft and six crews being ready to deploy overseas to offer global support to UK or Coalition forces anywhere in the world."

Opposite: Nimrod of the future – the BAE Systems Nimrod MRA4. The original airframes have been stripped down and completely rebuilt and the aircraft has been packed with the latest mission suites and avionics technology.
Photograph courtesy of BAE Systems

HEAVY METAL
Transport and Tankers

The RAF's transport and tanker aircraft provide vital support for UK armed forces. They haul freight, and they transport personnel, as well as acting as airborne fuel stations. These aircraft facilitate operations around the globe and to many are the unsung heroes of the RAF.

HERCULEAN FEATS

Lockheed Martin C-130 Hercules

The Royal Air Force has operated the Lockheed Martin C-130 Hercules since the first examples entered service in April 1967. These original C-130Ks (designated C1 and C3 in RAF service) have provided the backbone of the RAF strategic and tactical transport force ever since. By the early 1990s the heavy workload had taken its toll of these original aircraft and consequently 25 'next generation' C-130Js were ordered from Lockheed Martin. Two versions were ordered, the stretched C-130J, known by the RAF as the C4, and the standard J, known as the C5. The arrival of the first 'Js' meant the return of some early 'Ks' to the manufacturer for refurbishment and re-delivery to new customers, with the remaining examples being retained in RAF service for both tactical and strategic operations until the arrival of the new Airbus A400M.

The introduction of the J-model resulted in major restructuring plans for RAF Lyneham's operational squadrons, with No 24 Squadron becoming the first C-130J unit and initially responsible for strategic transport and the training role for the type. No 30 Squadron worked up as the second C-130J squadron from 2002 and is now responsible for tactical training. The hard work tradition of the Hercules community is known throughout the Service – RAF Lyneham's No 38 EAW (Air Transport) keeps the logistics moving, keeps the troops supplied and supports deployments. Indeed, Lyneham is also home to No 1 Air Mobility Wing that provides highly skilled air and surface movements support teams specialising in the loading and unloading of personnel and freight in any hostile or benign environment. It is these personnel who are working hard in testing environments such as the dust and heat of the desert in Afghanistan, including 'outside the

Previous pages, left: The RAF's Hercules force is operating to a hectic pace supporting forces in Afghanistan and Iraq, flying re-supply and communication missions and underlining their reputation as the RAF workhorses.

Previous pages, right: Photographed during a low-level tactical training mission from RAF Lyneham, a pair of C-130Js turn to make the next waypoint. The Lyneham Hercules crews are as at home flying medium-level long-distance strategic transport missions as they are operating low-level tactical operations.

Right: With Mk4 helmets donned, the crew of a C-130J from No 30 Squadron at Lyneham prepare for a tactical training sortie in Wales. The operational tempo of the Hercules fleet means that standard squadron training has to be carefully planned around combat support commitments.

Above: Escorted into RAF Mount Pleasant by two No 1435 Flight Tornado F3s, a Lyneham Transport Wing Hercules C3 arrives in the Falkland Islands. The station was opened here formally in 1984 to establish a fighter and transport presence in the Islands following the Falklands Conflict. As well as the four Tornados, a single VC10 tanker and Hercules are maintained here on a rotational basis by No 1312 Flight as well as two Sea Kings. *Photograph by Mike Jorgensen*

Opposite, far left: The C-130J's two pilots make use of an advanced Flight Management System (FMS) and Head Up Display (HUD), as well as a fully digital cockpit.

Opposite, left: Green on!! Go! Go! A paratrooper exits the side 'para door' of an RAF Hercules. *Photograph by Derek Bower*

wire' operations wearing body armour and helmets, working on engine running offloads in extremely dangerous conditions.

Lyneham's Hercules crews are as at home flying medium-level, long-distance strategic transport missions as they are operating low-level tactical operations into rough desert airstrips at night on Night Vision Goggles (NVGs). Crews are capable of flying six-ship formation missions into drop zones behind enemy lines to dispatch paratroopers and 'wedge' loads from the ramp of the aircraft at night and at low level. The RAF's Hercules have been operating in Afghanistan and Iraq ever since the current Operations 'Herrick' and 'Telic' started – flying daily re-supply and communication missions and underlining their reputation as the RAF workhorses.

Initially, No 24 Squadron had a number of necessary constraints with the new C-130Js when they were introduced into service. Strategic, rather than tactical, missions became the normal tasking, routing vital supplies and equipment to the Persian Gulf via Cyprus

to support British forces in the region. As tactical operational clearances were approved, the C-130J began to spread its wings and was soon operating alongside the C-130K across a full range of tactical transport support operations.

One pilot commented, "It is such a different method of operation over the first generation Hercules. Instead of a four-man flight deck, we've got a three-man crew. This means that the crew operation is very different. You've got a mass of information available and you need to manage it. Apart from the control column and the windows, the cockpit is completely different. The C-130J has proven to be more effective than the older K in some areas, particularly where hot and high operations are warranted. A good example of this was in Afghanistan during 2002, when, because of the high altitude of Kabul and the relatively large amount of fuel required to get to Thumrait, the J-model could offer a 12 tonne payload whereas the K model could only offer 7 tonnes. These figures were derived using Normal Operating Standard for the J, whereas the K had to use the more extreme Military Operating Standard to justify its payload – in short, higher risk for less capability.

The most noticeable changes to the fleet have come as we have increased our experience and received operating clearances to match. The whole arena of tactical, NVG and low-level operations has been constantly developing. To a large extent the improvements in navigational accuracy and ease of operating in a two-pilot flight deck with a Flight Management System (FMS) are taken for granted by the crews now. The one thing that everyone comments on is how quiet it is on the flight deck at high workload times, when the K model flight deck would have been buzzing with the constant drone of information being passed between the navigator and the pilots. Similarly, the throttles and carefree engine handling are normal for us now and the thought of having no Head Up Display (HUD) is frankly appalling."

Sqn Ldr Mark Pearce served on the C-130J Tactical Training Flight at No 30 Squadron, with the unit conducting tactical-flying and post-graduate training for

the C-130J. "We are aiming to train an equal number of crews on the tactical aspects of flying the C-130J on both Nos 24 and 30 Squadrons. The C-130J offers great situational awareness to pilots as it has a lot of equipment to let you know exactly what is going on at any one time. You can effectively have one guy doing a lot of work on the radios for example and the other pilot will be flying the aircraft, knowing exactly where, when and how the mission is going. We are taking the C-130J into combat theatres and 12 aircraft in the fleet are to have a full Defensive Aids System fitted. These aircraft are busy doing route flying, but a lot of the places we're going to are hostile areas and you really need these defensive systems. We have looked at a lot of the threats and worked out how we are going to fly our missions."

Flt Lt Steve Forster is a C-130J pilot: "I flew nine years on the C-130K. The C-130J is more of a pilot's aeroplane as you don't have a navigator or a flight engineer, so it really concentrates the mind. The loadmaster has picked up a lot of what the navigator and the engineer used to do in the cockpit, certainly in terms of lookout and managing the fuel panel. The tactical flying is outstanding in the C-130J. When we start the mission-planning phase we have a lead crew and a follower, possibly more with a bigger formation. One of the lead crews will plan the mission and brief it. The JAMPA (PC-based C-130J Advanced Mission Planning Aid) downloads to a ruggedised PC card which is then plugged into the aircraft." Flt Lt Dave Stewart, another C-130J pilot, gave more details on the tactical operations of the C-130J. "We have never flown with navigators on the C-130J and don't have any on the squadrons. When it comes to Tactical 'Tac' training, our guys start at a much higher workload to get them used to the demands put on them by changes in routings and intelligence/air picture scenarios. Indeed, the very first flight on the 'Tac' course involves airborne re-routes and changes of targets and timings. The computers really do make that much slicker than the old pen on a map."

The two C-130K squadrons, Nos 47 and 70, fly three C1s with the remainder being C3 or C3As. The C3A has

the Northrop Grumman NEMESIS Directional Infra-red Countermeasures self-protection system fitted. No 47 Squadron supports Special Forces operations, while No 70 Squadron gives tactical support to 16 Air Assault Brigade. No 70 Squadron also has an embedded Tactical Training Flight responsible for strategic transport and training.

The future for RAF air transport is certainly challenging as it is required to match available resources to the current extremely high operational tempo. Retirement of the C-130Ks is entirely dependent on the arrival of the new Airbus A400M transport aircraft. A400M will bridge the capability gap between the strategic-lift capacity of the C-17 and the tactical capacity of the C-130J.

Above: The Home of the Hercules – a No 24 Squadron C-130J overflies Lyneham.

Opposite: The first-generation RAF Hercules C3s have been fitted with some highly effective new mission equipment including low-light TV cameras, Forward Looking Infra-Red and advanced self-protection systems to help support their Special Forces mission. *Photograph by Richard Cooper*

TAC Comms

Tactical Air Traffic Control (Tac ATC) is part of the Tactical Communications Wing based at RAF Brize Norton. The specialist nature of their role results in frequent deployments for the men and women of the Unit, be it on exercise or on operations supporting the RAF from austere airstrips with little or no facilities. One member of the Tac ATC team, Flt Lt Gez Currie, described the challenges associated with working in a theatre of operation like Afghanistan. "The working conditions out by the tactical landing strip are some of the hottest we've worked in, regularly above 45 degrees. The unusually fine sand has also proved to be an issue since it is much finer than that seen in the UK and is whipped up by the afternoon's strong winds. Everything, including personnel, has to remain well covered." Flt Lt Currie's two-man team is also used to travelling light, operating with the minimum equipment required to ensure that the landing strip or airfield can be operated safely, day or night. Sergeant Steve Hutchings said, "We operate with what we can carry, we don't need a huge amount of space and we operate with the minimum of kit. We carry communications equipment that allows us to speak to aircraft; lights and fluorescent panels to mark the Temporary Landing Zone in poor visibility; and NVGs to enable operations at night. We also carry a portable weather station, but that's pretty much all we need to ensure that aircraft can operate tactically and safely, even from the most remote of strips."

TAC Medical Wing

Tactical Medical Wing (TMW) trains and deploys RAF medical personnel and units throughout the world, in peacetime and during periods of crisis. TMW was formed on 1 April 1996 at RAF Lyneham, which acts as the 'operational hub' for all personnel of the RAF Medical Services and relies heavily on a handful of specialist personnel, including RAF Regiment Gunners, Suppliers and Technicians as well as the Royal Auxiliary Air Force (RAuxAF). The RAF also stations highly trained medical personnel at bases across the country.

Above: A tactical communications officer at work with Hercules on a tactical landing strip. The team travels light and is responsible for ensuring the landing strip or airfield can be operated safely, day or night. *Photograph by Derek Bower*

Right: The RAF air transport fleet never rests. The RAF Boeing C-17A Globemaster force is pivotal to the RAF military heavy-lift capability. The C-17 is agile and effective, and is clearly very popular with the personnel that operate it at No 99 Squadron at RAF Brize Norton.

GLOBAL PRESENCE

Boeing C-17A Globemaster III

The RAF Boeing C-17A Globemasters of No 99 Squadron at RAF Brize Norton have provided a dramatic improvement in strategic heavy-lift capability. The C-17 is a state-of-the-art airlifter, and is as agile as a much smaller, fly-by-wire aircraft. It meets all of the RAF's requirements comfortably. When the MoD needs to haul huge loads over long distances to support deployed forces it can call on No 99 Squadron's C-17s – they are worth their weight in gold. Master Aircrew

Spike Abbott, an experienced loadmaster on the Unit, explained why. "We are currently covering both operational theatres of 'Telic' in Iraq and 'Herrick' in Afghanistan. These are continuously served by a C-17 crew that is forward-based in Al Udeid, Qatar, and Incirlik, Turkey, on a ten-day detachment during which they perform two shuttles into theatre, first into Afghanistan and then into Basra, Iraq, before heading back to Brize Norton. We tend to go into theatre at night with the two pilots and the loadmaster up in the cockpit using NVGs. Typically, the 'Bullet' aircraft comes out from Brize Norton with a load aboard. The resident crew then take it into theatre and after offload immediately come back, so the aircraft isn't sitting out and vulnerable in an operational area. We tend to find ourselves hauling loads that include Chinook, Apache or Puma helicopters, as well as ammunition, passengers and supplies for the deployed forces. Our normal seating allows for 54 passengers, but we can accommodate a full 102-passenger load by using stowed seats that can be fitted into the centre of the deck in about 30 minutes.

The role of the loadmaster is extremely important for the C-17 operation. We fly with a three-man crew, two pilots and a loadmaster, but we also carry a ground engineer and a servicing crewmember. As a loadmaster I have a diverse role on the C-17. As well as looking after the load, I am also tasked with working some of the radios and gathering weather information for the flight ahead – so I am always working hard and basically looking after absolutely everything from the flight deck back. The aircraft load will have already been allocated to the aircraft by the C-17 supervisor,

Above right: Master Aircrew Spike Abbott is an experienced Loadmaster on No 99 Squadron at RAF Brize Norton. The C-17 force is currently highly involved with supporting the operational theatres of 'Telic' in Iraq and 'Herrick' in Afghanistan.

Right: As day turns to night, movement staff at No 99 Squadron work to unload a Royal Marines Lynx helicopter from a C-17A.

who is one of the movement staff; they plan what we will take and exactly where we will load it. The loadmaster then plans and supervises the actual loading onboard. It is very straightforward because the C-17 was purpose-built for the job. When they designed the main hold, they spoke to loadmasters to make sure they got it absolutely right.

All C-17 aircrews do their initial training at Altus AFB, Oklahoma. The loadmasters do three months out there and a further three months training back here with our own training flight. The aircrew do two months of simulator training at Altus before coming back here for the live-flying phase of their course. We have lots of guys re-roling from Hercules, as well as new aircrews coming from ab initio training. By 2008 we will have six aircraft as we increase the fleet and this will inevitably see our taskings going up. But we are always desperate for new manpower; ever since we brought the initial four aircraft into service everyone has wanted us to support them."

Above: No 99 Squadron aircrew and groundcrew conduct initial training alongside USAF C-17 colleagues at Altus AFB in the USA. The cockpit of the C-17 is configured much like a fighter, with central stick control grip and Head Up Display (HUD).

Left: The cavernous C-17 is a most versatile strategic transport aircraft and can deliver outsized loads into small austere airfields with runways as short as 4,000ft (1,220m). No 99 Squadron's C-17s are the new 'Block 12' version of the airlifter; these aircraft are equipped with upgraded software and avionics and have additional fuel tanks that extend the aircraft's 2,500 (4,630km) nautical mile range by some 15 per cent.

STRONG SUPPORT

Vickers VC10

RAF Brize Norton in Oxfordshire is all about the tanker and medium transport fleet of VC10s and TriStars. The VC10 fleet is the backbone of the RAF strategic tanking force and the flexibility of operations that the type affords is immeasurable. The team at No 101 Squadron fulfil a plethora of deployment requirements and support duties literally around the globe, playing key roles in supporting assets during Operations 'Herrick' and 'Telic'. Indeed, the RAF forward-deploys VC10s to specifically support air assets in action in the skies over Iraq monitoring the ground situation. The VC10s are on hand to provide valuable refuelling in mid-air to extend the time fighters and surveillance aircraft can spend 'watching' the forces below.

The VC10 fleet is old, but the airframes are strong and reliable. Having first entered service in 1966, the oldest RAF examples are the C1Ks. The VC10 C1K can be configured for air transport as well as air-to-air refuelling (AAR) – for troop carrying it can carry 124 passengers as well as its nine crew – or it can be configured as a dual-role passenger/freighter. The aircraft can also be used for aeromedical evacuation, for which up to 68 stretchers may be fitted. The C1Ks were converted to the AAR role in 1993 through the addition of Mk32 refuelling pods under the outboard wings.

The bulk of the RAF's single-role AAR fleet comprises VC10s of two different variants, the K3 and K4. In 1978 the RAF contracted BAE Systems to convert five ex-BOAC (via Gulf Air) VC10s and four ex-East African Airways Super VC10s as AAR tankers. These were known in service as the K2s and K3s. This was followed in 1981 when 14 ex-British Airways Super VC10s were purchased and used for spares. In the early 1990s, five of the aircraft were revived and converted to K4 tankers. Each aircraft is a three-point tanker, with fuel being dispensed from the two wing-hoses or from the single fuselage-mounted Hose Drum Unit (HDU). The wing hoses can transfer fuel at up to 1,000kg (2,205lb) per minute and are used to refuel tactical

Above: The main element of the RAF's air-to-air refuelling fleet are the VC10 K3 and K4 variants. These versions of the VC10 are configured as three-point tankers with fuel offloaded to receiver aircraft via two wing-hoses or from the single fuselage-mounted Hose Drum Unit (HDU), usually reserved for larger aircraft.

Left: The VC10 can also receive fuel – as illustrated here – from another VC10 or TriStar with its air-to-air refuelling probe, which is permanently attached to the aircraft nose.

Photograph by Mike Jorgensen

fast-jet aircraft. The HDU can transfer fuel up to 2000kg (4,410lb) per minute and is usually used to refuel 'heavy' strategic aircraft, although it can also be used by fast-jet aircraft.

The VC10 is now reaching the end of its service life, but continual modifications maintain the aircraft as a significant asset, enabling the rapid deployment of troops and their weaponry, and fast-jet fighter aircraft, to any theatre of operations around the world.

Above: The Vickers VC10 has been in service with the RAF since 1966, and No 101 Squadron marked the 40th anniversary for the type in 2006. The previous operator of the original C1K variant was No 10 Squadron, now disbanded to concentrate all VC10 operations with No 101 Squadron at RAF Brize Norton.

EVALUATING THE HEAVIES

Making the biggest better

The Air Transport and Air-to-Air Refuelling Operation Evaluation Unit is tasked with enhancing the operational capabilities of the RAF tanker transport force through the provision of trained personnel to conduct tactical development and operational evaluation.

Above and right: The VC10 aircraft is equipped with a modern flight-management system and the avionics required for full worldwide operations. The crew comprises two pilots, a weapon systems officer, a flight engineer, an air loadmaster and up to three air stewards.

Above: Built to last – the old but effective maze of dials and
switches on the main console in the VC10 cockpit.
The well-worn throttle quadrant reveals the age of the
popular VC10.

ROYAL MISSION

Red carpet treatment

No 32 (The Royal) Squadron operates a mixed fleet of VIP-configured aircraft that are stationed at RAF Northolt in West London. The Squadron flies the HS125 CC3 and a pair of BAE 146 CC2s as well as three AgustaWestland A109 helicopters for Royal and VIP transport duties and in direct support of operations worldwide. The operational role of the Squadron has increased year on year and it is now tasked to provide two aircraft in-theatre on operations throughout the year. The increased presence of British Forces in the Afghanistan Theatre in particular is giving the detachment a considerable amount of tasking into Kabul, Kandahar and Bagram, transporting key decision-makers and equipment in support of ongoing operations. Also at Northolt, the Station Flight operates a pair of BN-2T Islander CC2s in the photographic mapping and light communications roles, with the aircraft able to be re-roled to passenger or freight configuration.

Lockheed Martin TriStar

Across the airfield at Brize Norton is No 216 Squadron. Its fleet of TriStars work alongside the VC10s and are adapted for the tanker role as well as for cargo and 'trooping' roles. The type regularly flies long-haul routes to destinations such as the Falkland Islands and North America. The TriStars were acquired from British Airways and Pan-Am as a direct result of lessons learnt in the Falklands Conflict. The need for long-range tanker assets with an additional capability to routinely operate to the South Atlantic led to the purchase.

No 216 Squadron stood up in November 1984 with the TriStars procured as dual-role tanker/transports. The Squadron has subsequently played a key role in many of the UK's operations, including Operation 'Allied Force', in Kosovo, with three aircraft based in Italy in support of NATO aircraft. The mixed fleet of nine aircraft include six modified by Marshall of Cambridge as tanker aircraft, with a twin, centreline hose-and-drogue configuration. Four aircraft were designated KC1, while two were designated K1. On a typical AAR flight from the UK to Cyprus, or across the Atlantic, the KC1 can refuel up to four fast-jet aircraft and simultaneously carry up to 31 tonnes of passengers and/or freight. The addition of a large, fuselage freight-door and a roller-conveyor system allows outsized palletised cargo to be carried.

Both VC10 and TriStar fleets are slated to be directly replaced by the new FSTA – Future Strategic Tanker

Above: Much more than just a 'Royal Flight' – No 32 (The Royal) Squadron operates a mixed fleet and spends much of its time supporting deployed operations. *Photograph: Crown Copyright*

Aircraft – early in the next decade. In 2003, the European consortium AirTanker Ltd was chosen by the UK Ministry of Defence as the preferred bidder for FSTA, putting the Boeing-led TTSC (Tanker Transport Services Company) team out of the frame. The winning A330-200 proposal was given the green light to move into a contract development and negotiation phase to ensure that the proposal meets all MoD requirements. If AirTanker can fulfil these requirements, it will mean that the proposed PFI (Private Finance Initiative) is the preferred way forward for the MoD, and AirTanker will get the full £13bn contract to supply 14 A330-200s over a planned 27-year contract. The RAF will retain responsibility for all military tasks, whilst AirTanker will own, manage and maintain the aircraft and also provide infrastructure and support and some training facilities. The new aircraft will be stationed at RAF Brize Norton.

Above: No 216 Squadron at RAF Brize Norton operates the versatile Lockheed Martin TriStar in the tanker/transport role.

Photograph by Derek Bower

Right: RAF TriStars have received a comprehensive avionics suite, which is undergoing further modernisation. The K1 and KC1 tankers are also fitted with the Joint Tactical Information Distribution System.

Opposite above: RAF TriStars are heavily involved with supply and troop missions into the most dangerous of operational theatres. Consequently they have been fitted with the latest Large Aircraft Infra-red Countermeasures system to help protect them from hostile ground fire.

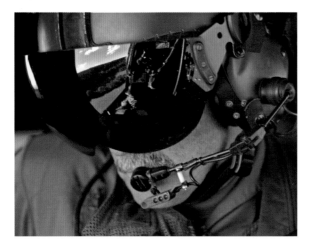

HELICOPTER HEROES
Support Helicopters and Search and Rescue

The RAF Support Helicopter (SH) force, which operates under the overarching control of the tri-Service Joint Helicopter Command (JHC), is undoubtedly one of the busiest branches of the Service as it enters its 90th year. When it comes to reacting to world crises, supporting ground forces through re-supply, or providing support cover and getting the troops in and out of hotspots, the RAF's helicopters are never far away. In recent years the RAF's helicopters and the men and women that work on them have maintained a footprint in all major UK military operations around the globe – offering extraordinary levels of professionalism and service despite ever-increasing commitments and strains on its fleet. As with all RAF branches, the SH force is a 'can do' force.

REJOICING IN FLIGHT

Defence Helicopter Flying School

Starting out in the arena of helicopter flying requires very specialised training. Recruitment for the field of rotary operations is hotly contested, with many new RAF personnel keen to progress onto helicopters due to the challenges offered. The Defence Helicopter Flying School (DHFS) was established at RAF Shawbury in Shropshire in April 1997 to train helicopter pilots and rear crew for all three Services. Reporting to No 22 Training Group, it is the one-stop shop for all RAF helicopter training up to operational conversion and ultimately the front-line. The School is a military organisation with military management at all levels. However, a civilian contractor, FBHeliservices Ltd, provides and maintains a fleet of 27 Squirrel HT1s and 11 Griffin HT1s which, although contractor owned, are on the military register. Instruction to the students is given by an experienced team of serving and ex-Service instructors from all three Services.

After students have completed elementary fixed wing flying training, the DHFS utilises the Squirrel to conduct basic rotary training before RAF students progress to the Griffin HT1s of Sixty (R) Squadron for advanced training in multi-engine rotary operations, where they are joined by their RAF WSOp counterparts. On completion of this Griffin course, pilots and rear

Above: The Defence Helicopter Flying School basic helicopter trainer (the Eurocopter Squirrel HT1) at work near RAF Shawbury.

Opposite: No Sixty (R) Squadron teaches RAF helicopter pilots how to operate a large, multi-engine type, with its fleet of Griffin HT1s. The Squadron's experienced serving and ex-RAF instructors impart the knowledge necessary to take out to the demanding world of the front line. Two Griffins are also detached at RAF Valley with the Search and Rescue Training Unit (SARTU) to enable crews to learn the demanding techniques necessary for such flying. No 84 Squadron at RAF Akrotiri, Cyprus, also operates the Griffin in the SAR and battlefield support role.

Previous pages: The RAF SH force is swift to react to requirements, being rapidly deployable, adaptable and extremely well trained – as illustrated here by a Puma HC1 of No 33 Squadron. In the RAF's 90th year, support helicopters are out in combat theatres, getting shot at, ferrying troops, bringing in supplies – delivering capability.

crew move to their operational Units for front-line training on their specific types.

The DHFS is directly responsible for training new pilots and WSOps for the RAF in conjunction with their colleagues from the other two Services. Therefore, the approach is very much a joint ethic but reinforcing the ethos and traditions of the individual Services. Hence, an Army Air Corps (AAC) unit, 660 Sqn AAC, delivers Single Engine Basic Rotary Wing training with the Squirrel, and a Royal Navy training unit, 705 NAS, delivers Single Engine Advanced Rotary Wing training, also on the Squirrel. Finally, Sixty (R) Squadron RAF provides Multi Engine Advanced Rotary Wing (MEARW) training with the Griffin HT1. The Search and Rescue Training Unit (SARTU) is also part of DHFS but detached to work out of RAF Valley where the conditions are ideal to deliver the SAR and mountain flying training element of the MEARW syllabus.

Flt Lt Matthew Holloway is a new RAF student pilot on 705 NAS. "I spent four years on a University Air

Squadron before being streamed for helicopters. I started out at 660 Squadron before coming here to 705 NAS. The helicopter force is a very exciting place to be at the moment and I am hoping to move to the Merlin force and some very challenging flying. Our training is very much geared towards our future operations, and we have a lot of young enthusiastic people here with a lot to offer. I personally chose the RAF as a career because it's very exciting, especially in today's environment. We all have our own tailored interest but the chat here is very much about getting through the course. The learning curve is very steep – we go solo after 11 hrs, and the flying I have achieved so far is mind-boggling – but we take it step-by-step, flight-by-flight. The tri-Service environment here is very interesting, and all three Services have very unique ways of doing things, but we have a good environment to work in."

Captain Martin Westwood Royal Navy is Commandant of DHFS. "This school was formed ten years ago to streamline a process where the Services were training people in a very similar way but at three different locations. Ten years on and over 3,000 students later I can say, 'Yes, it works'. There is one syllabus that uses best practice from all the earlier regimes, and all three Services' helicopter pilots and RAF aircrewmen and women come here to train. This means about 180 ab initio pilots and 40 crewmen every year to meet the demands of the front line as well as about another 200 personnel on top of that who are returning to flying duties from other posts. It is big, busy and very much joint training where all three Services live, work and train together to the same standards. However, we maintain and push the individual Services' ethos, which is why we have the 'badged' squadrons. Our Private Finance Initiative format is also a success in the training environment. FBHeliservices is our partner; they own the aircraft, engineers and 40 per cent of the flying instructors, but they all fly to military standards and rules and I get the desired number of aircraft on the flightline every day. They also almost invariably remain serviceable all day as well – a clear benefit of a

partnership incentivised by output! To make sure we stay relevant, we talk constantly to Joint Helicopter Command (JHC), and the other Commands, to look at lessons from current operations and see how we can develop the syllabus to suit the front line. There is no doubt that the Support Helicopter Force is where it's happening, and the guys and girls from here know they will go almost straight onto operations when they graduate from operational conversion."

Above: A DHFS Eurocopter Squirrel HT1 and trainee crew practise uneven terrain landings at Chetwynd relief landing airfield.

COOL CAT

Puma HC1

Originally delivered to No 33 Squadron at RAF Odiham in 1971, the Anglo-French Westland Puma is a versatile and reliable platform for the RAF. The Puma fulfils many roles and has seen extensive service in Northern Ireland, where the type continues to maintain a support presence with No 230 Squadron. No 33 Squadron, now at RAF Benson in Oxfordshire, has a full operational role as well as performing operational type-conversion training. Until March 2003, No 33 Squadron was heavily involved in Operation 'Palatine', part of the NATO stabilisation force in Bosnia, and now has major niche involvement in Operation 'Telic'. The Squadron's detachment in Baghdad is a critical asset to forces in the Iraqi capital, with Squadron personnel

Above: The loadmaster performs final visual checks before the Puma 'lifts' from RAF Benson. Puma crews are engaged in highly specialised support missions in Baghdad and are regularly engaged in the demanding training required by these missions.

Left: Puma on the prowl – on a training mission from RAF Benson, a Westland Puma HC1 of No 33 Squadron charges along at tree-top level. The crew is working to split-second timings in a realistic scenario that includes simulating dropping off troops through fast roping, getting in and out of confined landing sites and instrument flying.

Above: Heading into London, a Puma HC1 of No 33 Squadron routes along the River Thames as the autumn weather closes in.

Right: When decisions are made at the very top of the command structure, it is the front line that reacts and carries out its taskings and orders. This image nicely illustrates this equation as a Puma of No 33 Squadron overflies the Houses of Parliament, with Westminster Abbey, Downing Street and Horse Guards Parade in the background.

deploying three times every year for two months at a time. One experienced WSOp crewman commented, "The Puma is extremely popular, it is the only helicopter of its size in RAF service and it is a simple design that is also very quiet. The troops particularly like working with us because we have two doors for the cabin, which makes us very versatile when we need to deploy troops quickly."

Flt Lt Sarah Furness is a pilot on the Squadron. "I have been flying the Puma for two years and we have a mix of experience levels here as the aircrews range from very new crews to very experienced people."

The Puma teams deployed on operations in Iraq are flying in arguably the most demanding environment on the planet. One pilot commented, "What could be more challenging than flying at night, in a thick dust cloud, with limited power, in formation...whilst being shot at!"

MERLIN MASTERS

Merlin HC3

The RAF's Merlin HC3s of No 28(AC) Squadron at RAF Benson marked a new generation for the support helicopter on entering service in 2001. The day/night capable multi-role Merlin incorporates state-of-the-art design and technology; 90 per cent of the fuselage is made of composite materials and it incorporates a high level of redundancy in most of its vital components. Sgt Steve Thomas is a crewman on No 28(AC) Squadron and has been heavily involved in deployments with the Unit to Basra in Iraq, supporting the UK forces in the area with No 1419 Flight, operating in a high-threat environment. "I came to the Merlin directly from training at DHFS. The Merlin is a spacious and comfortable 'cab' and it is very popular with our crews and passengers alike. The troops we ferry around in

Left: Developed from a 1978 UK MoD requirement for a Sea King replacement as the EH101, the Merlin HC3 was selected by the RAF in 1993 as a new tactical battlefield support helicopter. No 28(AC) Squadron at RAF Benson operates 22 Merlins, with the force set to be boosted by a further six aircraft which will operate with No 78 Squadron here.

Above: The view of a Merlin at rest through NVGs.

Theatre find the Merlin far less fatiguing than other types as we have an active rotor head that dramatically reduces vibration. Merlin also has excellent air conditioning that keeps the cabin reasonably cool in the hot and high conditions and also removes much of the normal helicopter smells – dramatically helping reduce nausea for our passengers." In 2007 the RAF established a second Merlin unit at Benson, No 78 Squadron, which will operate six additional Merlin HC3As that were acquired under an urgent requirement from Denmark to deliver a rapid increase in helicopters for operations.

This underlined just how important the battlefield support helicopter has become for the modern RAF. Wg Cdr Nigel Colman, the new OC for No 78 Squadron, said, "28 Squadron is already the largest squadron in the Joint Helicopter Command with 22 aircraft and approximately 300 personnel. We are training crews at present for the new Squadron and will split the existing Merlins between the two Squadrons. The HC3As are like our HC3s but with enhancements such as new rotors and greater range, speed and lift, improving the capability still further".

Above: As day turns to night, Merlin crews can don NVGs and operate around the clock. This example flies at sunset with an underslung Land Rover.

Above: The Merlin HC3 features a variable speed cargo winch and roller conveyor for cargo handling, SAR hoist to starboard and cargo hook for external loads.

Opposite: A Merlin HC3 of No 28(AC) Squadron powers along at low level, the prime operating domain for support helicopters to evade ground fire. The Merlin features an integrated defensive aids system including Nemesis directional IR countermeasures, AN/AVR-2A(V) laser warning and Sky Guardian 200 radar.

Left: No 28(AC) Squadron officially re-formed on 17 July 2001 as the RAF Merlin squadron. A new Medium Support Helicopter Aircrew Training Facility, with two Merlin simulators, opened at Benson on 17 July 2000. The 22nd and final HC3 was handed over in November 2002. Full operational capability was attained by the Unit in early 2003 in time for the Merlins to deploy to Bosnia later that year.

Above: A Merlin conducts mountain-flying training in Snowdonia, North Wales. The helicopter is capable of carrying a long-wheelbase Land Rover and troops can board and strap-in within two minutes.

Left: The Merlin HC3 cockpit layout was revised from the original concept to better suit low-level operations. Each aircraft has provision for rapid installation of a chin-mounted FLIR turret and a refuelling probe beneath the nose.

This page: The call comes from the cockpit that the landing site is two minutes away – troops in the cabin prepare to stream out and take up defensive positions as the Merlin cleans up and clears out. The RAF Merlin operates with a standard crew of two pilots and loadmaster and an optional fourth crewman as dictated by the operational environment. In addition, the Merlin accommodates 24 fully armed troops on crashworthy seats. For defensive or supporting fire, provision is made for a pintle-mounted machine gun in the front side doors or the back ramp. RAF Merlins have seen action in Iraq since 2005 with No 1419 Flight in Basra, operating in multi-role configuration for Special Forces support, combat search-and-rescue, medical evacuation and as an airborne command post. In the first 800 hours of flight time recorded on deployment the Merlins achieved an impressive 89 per cent serviceability record.

Photograph above by Patrick Allen

Above: Still wearing markings from its previous tenure with No 78 Squadron in the Falkland Islands, this Chinook HC2 is operated by a No 27 Squadron crew on a confined area training exercise from RAF Odiham. The Squadron has recently played key roles in Operation 'Maturin' for humanitarian earthquake relief in Pakistan and Operation 'Highbrow', assisting with the evacuation of British and foreign nationals from Lebanon.

FURTHER, FASTER, HEAVIER

Boeing Chinook HC2

The Boeing Chinook HC2s based at RAF Odiham in Hampshire offer the RAF unprecedented levels of battlefield lift and support for troops on the ground. Whether operating from assault ships, dusty strips, in jungle clearings, or on remote hilltops, the Chinooks are versatile heavy lifters. Today, the three squadrons at Odiham are very much focused towards Afghanistan and Operation 'Herrick'. As operations officer at No 27 Squadron Flt Lt Mark Goodwin said, "We are very much focused on projection in Afghanistan right now and geared towards supporting the troops on the ground. No 27 Squadron is split into three flights and the day-to-day running of the Unit is geared towards supporting the current deployed force and preparing personnel for the next deployment."

A typical training mission in the UK replicates an Afghanistan scenario to prepare its crewmembers. The standard mission crew is two pilots and two air loadmaster crewmen; however, this can be increased to three crewmen if required. The main threats being encountered by the Chinooks in Afghanistan from the Taliban are small-arms fire, rocket-propelled grenades and some man-portable SAMs. It is all about tactical flying, low and fast, into the landing zone and out as quickly as possible. These crews are proud to support the troops on the ground, who are operating right in the front of the firing line.

Flt Lt Rich Millard-Smith is a seasoned Chinook pilot. "I've been on No 27 Squadron for five years having transferred from the Army Air Corps. The Chinook force has been working to a hectic tempo since I joined, first during the combat phase of Operation 'Telic' in 2003 before we were relieved by the Merlins; then, following a relative period of stability to re-group with consolidation training, we started Operation 'Herrick' in 2006. Despite our 'lull' in operations we still played key roles in humanitarian relief work for the Pakistan earthquake and the evacuation of citizens from Lebanon. We also took part in other overseas

Left: Chinooks from Odiham have been supporting Operation 'Herrick' in Afghanistan since 2006. The missions in Afghanistan are extremely demanding, non-stop, around the clock and in the face of a significant ground threat. A typical day for the crews might include re-supply missions, a medical evacuation from the middle of a battle, or transporting troops and humanitarian aid across the region. *Photograph by Patrick Allen*

Below: The standard mission crew for the Chinook is two pilots and two air loadmasters; however, this can be increased to three if required. The pilots and loadmasters work as a well-oiled team – able to complement each other and facilitate low, fast, tactical flying – getting into and out of a landing zone as quickly as possible.

commitments for operations and training, such as our regular deployments to Morocco for hot-and-high training. The missions in Afghanistan are extremely demanding. We are flying non-stop, around the clock and we face a significant threat from the Taliban. Our maintainers work solidly 24/7 to keep the 'cabs' in the air and it has become very wearing on everyone to maintain our presence. However, we are operating what I can only describe as an awesome aircraft in the Chinook. It has immense power and surprising agility for such a big helicopter. The Army call us their 'battlefield helicopter of choice' as we can lug personnel and equipment into locations that others simply can't reach. In Afghanistan we fight by Flight – deploying our squadron Flights on a rotational basis – the Airborne Reaction Force (ARF) and the High Readiness Force (HRF). The latter has medics aboard to enable a swift reaction to support our troops if they get into difficulties. The ARF has additional troops aboard, ready to swing into action to support our ground forces. These roles involve all of our Chinooks based in the region and they are available 24 hours a day, seven days a week. We also keep aircraft for taskings out of Kandahar and around Helmand Province.

Our deployment training starts around 16 weeks prior to departure from the UK. We start working with the Army unit that we will be out there supporting and we also start training with the latest defensive aids systems and practise our dust landings. We have a constant flow of new guys on the Squadron so our training commitments are vital. The Chinook force cannot overlook its UK training commitments as they are essential to ensure that the force can meet its requirements in Afghanistan. It is clearly a highly-demanding environment but our personnel are working hard and achieving incredible feats. They are the backbone of the support helicopter force and work tirelessly to ensure that the force delivers effective support time and time again."

Across the flightline at Odiham, No 18(B) Squadron also operates three flights, with one flight being the OCF (Operational Conversion Flight), while No 7

Squadron is dedicated to supporting UK Special Forces. Like the Merlin, the future for the Chinook force sees expansion through the arrival of the delayed HC3 variants that will be delivered to a specification to match the current force and allow a streamlined fleet increase to help meet its huge, unprecedented, operational commitments.

RESERVE FORCES

Support and Assistance

RAF Reserve forces make a valuable overall contribution to UK force levels and comprise the RAF Reserve (RAFR) and the Royal Auxiliary Air Force (RAuxAF). They operate alongside their regular Service colleagues and offer vital support and assistance to the SH force, both in the UK and when overseas on deployed operations. Members of the RAFR are normally individuals who are recruited for full or part-time service to provide support to the RAF in both peacetime and crisis. The RAuxAF, on the other hand, comprises volunteers who are mainly in full-time civilian employment. The RAuxAF celebrated its 80th Anniversary in 2004 and the organisation is as important today as it ever was – it offers excellent levels of service and represents exceptional value for money. Recent operations in Iraq and Afghanistan have demonstrated just how vital the RAuxAF's contribution can be to the Service and it has evolved from being an occasionally useful addition to the RAF front line to becoming an essential part of it. As the size of the regular RAF is reduced, the RAuxAF is playing an increasing role in not only meeting the commitments of the SH force, but to the wider RAF as a whole.

Above left: A Chinook over Camp Bastion in the middle of the desert in Helmand Province, Afghanistan. The Chinooks are attached to No 1310 Flight based alongside Army Air Corps Apache and Lynx helicopters of Joint Helicopter Force (Afghanistan), based mainly at Kandahar and Bastion. The Chinooks are escorted by Apache AH1s for protection from enemy forces on the ground. *Photograph by Patrick Allen*

Left: The Chinook offers immense power and surprising agility for such a big helicopter. The force prides itself on being able to carry personnel and equipment into locations that others simply cannot reach. *Photograph by Patrick Allen*

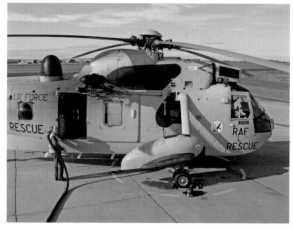

Above: The bright yellow Sea King HAR3/3As of the Search and Rescue (SAR) force are easily recognisable and work alongside the Coastguard and Royal Navy to provide coverage for over three million square miles of the UK.

Left: The seahorse badge on this Sea King HAR3 identifies this as a No 203(R) Squadron example.

RESCUE SQUAD

Westland Sea King HAR3

The bright yellow Sea Kings of the Search and Rescue (SAR) force are arguably the RAF's most renowned types and are responsible for a massive level of interaction with the general public due to their primary SAR role. The current fleet consists of two squadrons of Sea King HAR3/3As based at locations around the UK, working alongside the Coastguard and Royal Navy to provide coverage for over three million square miles. Rescues often call for crews to engage in extremely challenging flying in what can often be atrocious weather conditions.

Sqn Ldr Iain MacFarlane is a pilot with No 202 Squadron's 'D-Flight' at RAF Lossiemouth. "UK aeronautical SAR is co-ordinated by the Rescue Co-ordination Centre at RAF Kinloss, who look after SAR helicopters from three sources: the RAF, the Royal Navy and the Coastguard. The RAF has two squadrons, Nos 22 and 202. No 202 Squadron mainly covers the north of the UK, with No 22 covering the south. Each of the No 202 Squadron Flights at Lossiemouth, Boulmer and Leconfield and the No 22 Squadron Flights at Valley, Wattisham and Chivenor are commanded by a Squadron Leader and they each operate a pair of Sea Kings with five aircrews. The geographical location of each flight very much dictates the nature of the work that is expected. For example, Chivenor tends to pick up a lot of short-range rescues with holidaymakers who have got into trouble along the coastline, whereas here at Lossiemouth we predominantly work in the mountains as well as a smattering of jobs associated with the oil and fishing industries. Our biggest risk comes with the weather and it's a case of balancing those risks carefully against the benefits of completing the mission. We can battle through some fairly fearsome weather to get to casualties but often we drop off RAF Mountain Rescue teams so we can stay clear of the worst of the weather. This means that instead of hover taxiing up a mountain side into cloud, we might well drop the guys off and they'll stretcher the casualty back down to us for the ferry to hospital – so it's very much a team effort."

Despite being old aircraft, the Sea Kings are likely to remain in service until 2017, and the crews respect them as very effective rescue platforms. The SAR Sea Kings now feature new infra-red sensors with a zoom facility that, when allied with NVGs and radar, make the Sea King a potent search platform. The radar operator is known as the MSS (Multi-Systems Suite) operator, working alongside the standard crew of a captain and co-pilot. The MSS operator doubles up as winch operator at the scene of the rescue to work alongside the Winchman, who is medically trained to paramedic standard and actually goes down on the wire to work with the casualty.

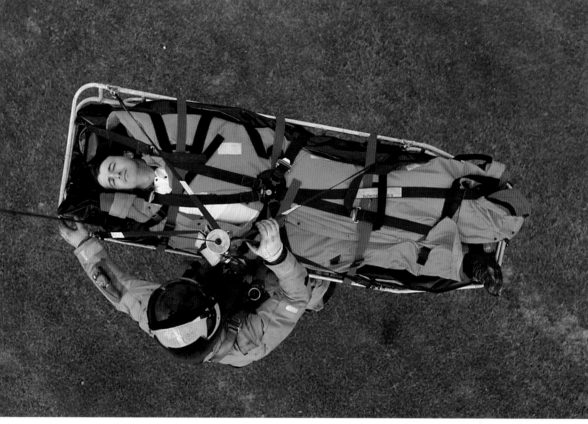

At RAF Valley, the Search and Rescue Training Unit gives new crews a basic grounding in SAR with its Griffin HT1s before they move onto No 203(R) Squadron – the OCU for the Sea King. Sqn Ldr Macfarlane continued. "I am relatively new to the SAR world, having joined in 2003 after 16 years on Chinooks. We get some very interesting taskings and when the bell rings, it all gets pretty exciting. When I was based at Boulmer, I was involved in the Carlisle floods where we spent nine hours rescuing people from the water. Up here I had to abandon an aircraft in the Cairngorms when we ran into particularly bad weather. Indeed, most of our memorable flying comes around the back of Ben Nevis in 50-60 kts of wind in the dark. By day we have 15 minutes to get airborne – but we usually manage it in quite a bit less than that. We have bedrooms on site and we have crews here 24 hours a day, ready to respond to any eventuality."

Above: Winchman and casualty.
Photograph by Derek Bower

Left: The SAR teams come to the rescue in all situations. Indeed an RAF Sea King from E Flight, No 202 Squadron, conducted a rescue in February 2007 when a Virgin Trains Express was derailed at Greyrigg in Cumbria.

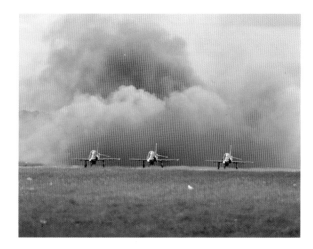

RAF ON DISPLAY
A Polished Performance

The public face of the RAF serves many valuable purposes. As well as helping with recruitment through air displays, RAF display teams help support UK industry overseas as they portray professionalism and capabilities that are of the highest order.

THE RED ARROWS

Royal Air Force Aerobatic Team

The Royal Air Force Aerobatic Team, the Red Arrows, represents the very public face of the RAF and serves to demonstrate the professionalism and excellence of the RAF and promote recruitment. When you watch the Red Arrows display, it is always polished, always executed with precision, and always very, very impressive.

Even before a display season ends, the team is preparing for the next season. Through winter and into spring the close-knit team of flying and support staff operate to a gruelling schedule – flying up to four times a day. It is not just about the pilots; the team is a squadron of 100 people who strive to represent the best that the Royal Air Force has to offer. Everyone in the Red Arrows team has a vital role to play and clearly everyone works with huge professionalism and pride.

To finely hone the skills of the team, the Red Arrows annually migrate to the popular RAF outpost at Akrotiri in Cyprus for intensive pre-season training, known as Springhawk, to make the most of the fine Mediterranean weather. Here the team embarks on an exhausting schedule of flying three full display practices every day of the working week to fine-tune the formation manoeuvres. The whole team works hard to ensure all the jets are on the line in the morning ready to make the most of the day's flying – every member of the team is working flat out to ensure the time spent in Cyprus is maximised.

In the air, the work rate for the pilots is extraordinary. The dark helmet visors of the nine pilots mask the immense concentration and workload necessary to stay on the wings of the leader as they paint the sky with red, white and blue smoke in their looping, rolling and breaking manoeuvres. 'Good show' comes the call from Red 10 on the ground as they complete the 'Vixen break', which is the finale of their show.

After over seven months of hard work in their pre-season training, both in Cyprus and the UK, the Red Arrows team are granted Public Display Authority, normally in mid-May of each year. This means that the team are ready and approved for the new season and geared up to wow the crowds once again. After the announcement is made, the whole squadron change into their red and blue flying suits to celebrate the official start of the new display season.

The Reds

Since mid-1966 there have been nine Red Arrows display pilots each year, including the team leader. Each year three new pilots, all volunteers, join the elite nine, but to be eligible to apply for the team they must have completed at least one operational tour on a front-line fast jet and have logged a minimum of 1,500 flying hours. Pilots must also have been assessed in their annual reports as being above average in their operational role as the usual three-year tour as a Red Arrows pilot is both physically and mentally challenging. For the pilots, it is some of the most exhilarating and skilful flying they will ever experience, but it is also very hard work. This ethos of hard work permeates through to the engineers and support staff as everyone on the team gives 100 per cent without fail.

The team leader and Officer Commanding (OC) for the 2007 season was Wg Cdr Jas Hawker (Red 1), who clearly has one of the most sought after, but most demanding, jobs in the world. The role of the formation leader is absolutely critical to the display and Wg Cdr Hawker is responsible for accurate positioning and precise timing throughout the complex routine. Each display venue is granted an airspace Temporary Restricted Area of six nautical miles (11km) radius based on the centre point of the display from the surface up to 8,500ft (2,590m). No other aircraft movement is permitted to enter that restricted area for the duration of the display. Therefore, it is the leader's responsibility to ensure that all of the manoeuvres are flown within the restricted airspace allotted to them. Red 1 leads the whole formation of nine aircraft for the first half of the

display, with a split at the halfway point into two groups. Red 1 continues to lead the front section (known as Enid), whilst the rear formation (known as Gypo) is led by Red 6, the Synchro Leader. The second half of the display contains manoeuvres which are much more dynamic, with the aim being to keep something happening in front of the crowd at all times.

On top of the rigours of display flying and practising (it is not unusual for Red Arrows pilots to fly four times a day!), the OC of the Red Arrows must also lead the whole Squadron as a fully functioning RAF unit. The job has been described as being similar to that of a Chief Executive of a medium-size company. Red 1 is responsible for a squadron of 100 people who strive to represent the best that the Royal Air Force has to offer.

As well as having total responsibility for the flying aspects of the job, he is also responsible for the welfare and well-being of all other members of the Red Arrows

and their families. To achieve these tasks, Wg Cdr Hawker can call upon a very strong management team with vast experience of life in the Royal Air Force. "The job of OC the Red Arrows is not just about leading the team during displays – it's about running a whole squadron. I love the job and I wouldn't change a single thing. The Circus groundcrews work very hard and come in at least two hours before the pilots to get the jets ready. In between sorties they are turning the jets around and when we go off to the hotel after a display they spend another two hours putting them away. The 2007 season was hard work because of the poor weather, not so much for the displays, but more during transit to and from the venues. Our 'flat' show can be completed with a 1,000ft cloudbase and just 3.5km visibility, but it's everything the public doesn't see that makes it difficult – for example the rejoins after formation splits become really tough in bad weather.

Above: Wg Cdr Dave Middleton (Wg Cdr RAFAT) chats with the team upon arrival at the Royal International Air Tattoo.

Top: Reds on the flightline between training.

Left and opposite: The Red Arrows place huge emphasis on formation perfection.

Previous pages, left: "Smoke on... Reds ready to roll".

Previous pages, right: "Reds break, break, GO!"

However, in 2007, in spite of the poor weather, we enjoyed some excellent displays in the UK, notably the spectacular venues at Windermere, Fowey Royal Regatta and Dartmouth Royal Regatta. Venues like these are very challenging for me as I have to get all nine aircraft safely down into the valley. This was a particular problem for our Swiss show in Bex, which is just to the south of Lake Geneva, with 7,000ft mountains all around the site. We had to modify the show significantly to ensure we could fly it safely. For example, normally we conduct some rejoins at 1,000ft, but due to the nature of the terrain at Bex we were sometimes rejoining up at 7,000ft – it was absolutely fantastic. We were flying down the valley with sheer granite either side of us and then looping with mountain tops above us.

As we moved into October, we were planning ahead for a tour of the Middle and Far East, which made for a busy end to the 2007 season. This meant that we had to keep the 2007 team up to display standard whilst working up for the 2008 season." But it doesn't end there; the 90th anniversary year of the RAF in 2008 will see the 'Reds' continuing to do their excellent work representing the UK and the Service with an additional planned tour to the USA and Canada. Charity work and fundraising forms a large part of the team's non-flying activities and they have achieved great success over the years. In addition to their intense flying schedule, the whole team is constantly involved in charity and community work – representing the Royal Air Force at home and around the world.

Many of the pilots and support staff have served on operational duties in Afghanistan and Iraq and many will be temporarily detached on operations overseas during their time with the Red Arrows. When they finally leave the team at the end of their three-year tour, both pilots and support staff will return to their normal mainstream duties, which directly support the RAF's operational commitments around the world.

The team's display schedule is directed by the RAF Participation Committee at HQ Air Command, based at RAF High Wycombe in Buckinghamshire, which has

responsibility for the allocation of all Royal Air Force display assets. All bids for RAF assets, including the Red Arrows, must be submitted by September each year for shows taking place in the following year. The Participation Committee review each application and attempt to dovetail all the RAF's display assets with the requests received. Many more requests are received than the RAF can possibly handle and the Participation Committee decides which displays can be carried out and which displays are operationally feasible. Display venues can be influenced by the requirements of the RAF's recruiting organisation; they may wish to target a particular area and would see a display by the Red Arrows as a positive aid to encouraging young people to consider a career in the Royal Air Force. The Red Arrows have a right of veto, but would normally only veto a display venue if, in the opinion of one of the senior pilots, the venue was considered to be unsafe.

The Red Arrows support team performs a vital 'behind-the-scenes' role in engineering, logistical support and public relations work. If the team is carrying out only one display at a particular venue on one day, support is limited to the engineers who fly in the back of each aircraft (only during transits and not during displays) as the Red Arrows administration and logistics staff at RAF Scampton will have already made arrangements with the host airfield for aircraft parking and refuelling facilities. According to Warrant Officer John May, the Team Adjutant, "If the team is scheduled to carry out more than one display on a given day, we will pre-position an enhanced team of engineers at the operating airfield. This small team will include five engineers whose primary task is to replenish the diesel/dye tank which generates the red, white and blue smoke so familiar to air display audiences across the world. If an overnight stay is required, support staff

Above: Nine aircraft engineering technicians are chosen to form a team known as Circus. Circus engineers are each allocated to a specific pilot for the duration of the summer display season and they fly in the back of the Hawks to and from display airfields to service the aircraft before and after every display. The unique experience of flying regularly in a fast jet means that these are some of the most sought-after engineering jobs in the RAF.

Above left: In close formation, upside down at 350kts (400mph) – the Reds in their element.

Opposite: Swooping over Lady's Mile beach, the Red Arrows practise near RAF Akrotiri, Cyprus.

will also have made arrangements for accommodation and transport for pilots and engineers as well as proper security for our aircraft."

Of course, the Red Arrows is not just about nine Hawks and nine pilots. Keeping the aircraft serviceable is a complex process for the 85 personnel of the team Engineering Flight – the Blues. The overall responsibility for the management of the Blues falls to the Senior and Junior Engineering Officers, these being Sqn Ldr Ed Williams and Flt Lt Allison Scott respectively in 2007. The Blues represent a cross-section of technical and non-technical trades, all combining to ensure the team completes its display programme. Nine of the Blues are chosen to form a team known as 'Circus' – they are aircraft technicians that directly support the pilots during the display season by servicing the aircraft before and after every display.

Above: The Red Arrows at work over the sea near RAF Akrotiri.

Left: Flt Lt Greg Perilleux pulls up hard during the 'Rollbacks'.

FLYING WITH THE REDS

From The Back Seat

It is a real privilege to be invited to fly with the 'Reds'. To help keep the team in the public eye they occasionally fly specialist aviation photographers or journalists as passengers on display practice sorties. Before flying with the team itself, first-time fliers get an essential check-out flight with Red 10 (Flt Lt Andy Robins) to make sure they can cope with the harsh environment that is the back seat of one of the nine team Hawks during the display. It is an onslaught of 30 minutes of gruelling aerobatic flying, and that is just for the passenger! Having cleared this hurdle, passengers 'walk' to the Hawks well in advance of the nine team pilots to ensure they are ready to make the exact slot times planned for the flights – there is no time for a

delay. The pilots don g-suits, life-saving jackets and helmets, and strap into the Hawks in very short order – ready to meet the required split second timing of the entire flight, which starts with a pre-determined check-in time. "Reds check, 2, 3, 4, 5, 6, 7, 8, 9." "Akrotiri tower, Red Arrows, nine aircraft ready to taxi." As 'The Boss' checks us in with the tower, I put my dark visor down and raise my oxygen mask as my pilot, Red 5, Flt Lt Damo Ellacott, checks I am ready to close the canopy. The MDC detonator cord in the canopy can potentially fire on closing the canopy so every care is taken when closing it in the Hawk. I have already dialled my weight into the ejector seat and lowered the seat to ensure I have a fist's worth of clearance above my white Mk10B helmet and the canopy. As we line up on the sunbleached runway, the adrenaline is already starting to flow – and I am just a passenger taking photos. "Display take-off coming left." The call from the leader comes as we line up at intervals along the runway. "Reds rolling...now." Power on, the pilots release the brakes and we roll as one. With my feet sitting lightly on the rudder pedals, the inputs come thick and fast from my pilot as he keeps the Hawk perfectly straight on the runway and in formation with the aircraft ahead. Once airborne the nine Hawks immediately move into tight diamond formation – this really is close, rock-solid formation flying and the pilots are all working incredibly hard. A balance of power, airbrake, rudder and stick are what these highly-skilled pilots use to hold this tight position and it is very impressive from my position as a passenger. We are cleared in to a flat practice display over the cliffs at Akrotiri. "Smoke on...go!" "Coming right...now." "Holding the bank...now." "Tightening." The calls from the front of the formation are constant and they are vital for the rest of the team, who are hanging on the leader's coat tails. The team leader has many factors to take into account to guide the team safely around the routine and ensure accurate positioning and precise timing. For this particular practice he also has a strong on-crowd wind to take into account. As a photographer passenger it is crucial that the pilot doesn't feel you in

the back; you never ever knock the control column by mistake, that could be inviting disaster. The 'tightening' call from the leader signals that g is coming on in the turn, only about 3g but enough to mean I need to brace or stow my Canon EOS1D camera up on the instrument panel coaming in front of me. "Letting it out." This call means that the leader is relaxing the pull in the turn and the g comes off. For the first half of the flat display it is a sequence of turns in changing formations, Typhoon, Concorde, Short Apollo to name a few. The work rate for the pilots is extraordinary throughout the entire flight. At what seems like just feet above the dark blue of the Mediterranean they are flying to the tightest of margins, lining up flap struts and other features on different parts of the aircraft in front to ensure perfect formation alignment.

As previously mentioned, the end of the first half of every display is marked by the team splitting into 'Enid' and 'Gypo' sections ready for the second, more dynamic half of the display. This involves a series of co-ordinated manoeuvres for the two sections including 'Gypo' section's famous 'Synchro' crossing manoeuvres, led by Red 6, the Synchro leader. After a sweat-soaked 30 minutes we are running in for the break over the runway. One last g-saturated pull and we are in sequence downwind for landing. A quick check from Damo that my toes are clear of the brakes and we turn finals to grease down on the runway at Akrotiri. The sweat is pouring off me, so goodness knows how the pilots have remained so cool. As we taxi in, I am cleared to replace my ejector seat and canopy safety pins and as we come to a halt, we are met by the dedicated groundcrews. As the canopy opens, the engines have already spooled down and Damo is climbing out. "See you inside," he says, as the engineers swing into action to prepare the jets for the next practice. The pilots immediately go into a detailed team debrief, making full use of the excellent video that is filmed from the ground for every display. This is a vital tool for the pilots and whilst watching the video they are very hard on themselves; calls of 'short', 'long', 'shallow', 'deep' from various members of the team

indicate how they feel their positioning was within each formation. Sitting in the debrief I struggle to see the errors, but these pilots are talking about literally inches of difference in positioning – hence the extraordinary levels of excellence the Red Arrows maintain throughout their display season. For me as a photographer it is a huge privilege and challenge to try to capture this incredible experience and give some insight into the team. In the words of the Red Arrows motto: 'Eclat' – brilliance.

Above: Coming over the top of the caterpillar manoeuvre.

Opposite: A smart red arrow adorns the team's flying helmets.

Left: The Typhoon roll.

Above: Low and fast, Reds 6 and 8 run in over the Akrotiri
cliffs for the 'Gypo pass'.

Right: Going vertical in the 'Champagne Split'.

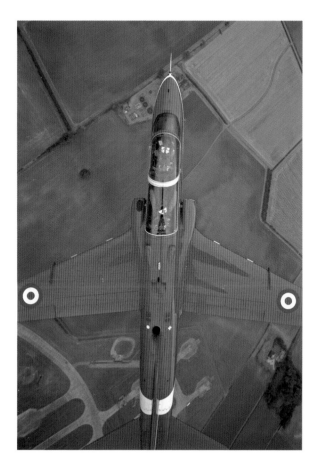

Above: The view from Red 7, looking down at Sqn Ldr Jim Turner (Red 6) in the 'Gypo Mirror Roll'.

Right: Red 6 inverted over the Scampton runway for the 'Corkscrew'.

Above: Coming out of a loop over home Station RAF Scampton – the incredible view from the backseat of Red 7.

Above: Diamond formation over the Akrotiri runway.

BATTLE OF BRITAIN

Battle of Britain Memorial Flight

The hangar doors clank shut behind them as the groundcrews push out a No 603 Squadron Supermarine Spitfire MkIIa by hand onto the grass dispersal in the summer morning air. The pilot climbs into the cockpit and in minutes the Rolls-Royce Merlin engine purrs into life. The elliptical-winged beauty is soon soaring towards the puffy cumulus clouds – in its element. This could easily be Hornchurch in 1940 and a fighter heading out to meet the marauding Luftwaffe. However, it is RAF Coningsby in 2007 and the Spitfire is heading for a flypast for the Battle of Britain Memorial Flight (BBMF). The Flight is the RAF's own living, breathing tribute to 'The Few' and arguably the RAF's 'Finest Hour'.

Few sights and sounds can be more evocative than the BBMF trio of Avro Lancaster, Supermarine Spitfire

Above: The Battle of Britain Memorial Flight.
Photograph by Geoffrey H. Lee

Left: Gp Capt Stuart Atha at the controls of the magnificent BBMF Spitfire MkIIa.

and Hawker Hurricane. These cherished aircraft are lovingly maintained by RAF groundcrews and flown by serving RAF pilots. In the years immediately following World War II it became traditional for a Spitfire and Hurricane to lead the Victory Day flypast over London. From that event there grew the idea to form an historic collection of flyable aircraft, initially to commemorate the RAF's major battle honour, the Battle of Britain, but in later years with a broader remit to commemorate the RAF's involvement in all the campaigns of WWII. In 1957 the Historic Aircraft Flight was formed at Biggin Hill, and in 2007 the Flight celebrated its 50th Anniversary.

Stationed today at RAF Coningsby in Lincolnshire, the Battle of Britain Memorial Flight is one of the world's best-known historic aircraft collections, maintaining an airworthy Lancaster I, five Spitfires of various marks, two Hurricanes, a Dakota III and two Chipmunks. Officer Commanding BBMF, Sqn Ldr Al Pinner, is the only aircrew member permanently serving on the Flight, the other pilots, navigators, air engineers and air loadmasters all come from different stations and fly everything from the Eurofighter Typhoon to the E-3D Sentry in their primary role. The aircrews give up effectively every other weekend from May to the end of September to fly and display the historic aircraft of the Flight.

The ethos of the Battle of Britain Memorial Flight is symptomatic of the history, service, pride and commitment that every member of the RAF shares. From 1918, to 1940, to 2008, every station, every squadron, every aircraft type, every person, occupies a very special part in its history. The ethos and sense of tradition that permeates throughout the RAF today is what helps make it function so well. This will undoubtedly continue in the years ahead, exactly as it has done for the past 90 years, thus helping to ensure the RAF of tomorrow remains as agile, as adaptable and as capable as our leaders demand.

Above: The BBMF is the RAF's own flying museum. The aircraft are maintained to the highest standard by the engineers.

Left: RAF classics representing the RAF through the ages: a Supermarine Spitfire MkIIa of the Battle of Britain Memorial Flight flown by Gp Capt Stuart Atha flies alongside a Eurofighter Typhoon F2 of No 29(R) Squadron flown by Flt Lt Antony Parkinson.

INDEX

Author Acknowledgements

The opportunity to produce *Fighting Force*, marking the 90th Anniversary of the Royal Air Force, has been a huge privilege. This book would not have been possible without the support, assistance and dedication of countless RAF personnel. I have named many people here, but there are many others behind the scenes who also made these photographs possible. To everyone, a massive 'thank you'. I hope I haven't overlooked anyone.

I would particularly like to thank Sqn Ldr Brian Handy from the Defence PR (RAF) Publications Office for all his work in helping arrange the complex issue of scheduling visits, as well as for his invaluable support in creating this book. I would like to thank Paul Turner and Sue Pressley at Touchstone Books for all their support and hard work to make this book look as fantastic as it does. I would also like to thank my partner Claire for all her encouragement and support.

The aerial images you see here were only possible thanks to the assistance of those who approve the flights, the doctors who declared me fit to fly, the flight safety equipment fitters, the dedicated engineers who prepared the aircraft and last, but not least, the skilled hands of the pilots. Without the aeroplane being in the right piece of sky I simply would not have been able to capture the right angles for the best photographs.

I would like to particularly thank:
ACM Sir Glenn Torpy, Chief of the Air Staff
Gp Capt Andy Bowen
Gp Capt Andrew Turner
Wg Cdr Ian Gale
Wg Cdr Tim Bullement
Dale Donovan, Air Command
RAF Henlow Centre of Aviation Medicine
No 100 Squadron, RAF Leeming
Flt Lt Anthony Horrigan
Phill O'Dell
Richard Cooper
Geoffrey H. Lee
Mike Jorgensen
Derek Bower
Patrick Allen

No 1 EFTS, RAF Cranwell

No 1 FTS, RAF Linton-on-Ouse
Flt Lt Matt Clarke
Flt Lt Jon Dunn
Flt Lt Tom Hill
Flt Lt Keren Watkins
Fg Off Nick Callinswood
Fg Off Andy York

No 4 FTS, RAF Valley
Gp Capt Tony Barmby, Station
    Commander
Wg Cdr Adrian Hill, OC No 19(R) Squadron
Wg Cdr Gary Kelly, OC No 208(R) Squadron
Sqn Ldr Mark Byrne
Flt Lt Alex Tennant
Flt Lt Keith 'Fruit Bat' Frewin
Fg Off Ben Durham
Survival Equipment Section RAF Valley

No 3 FTS, RAF Cranwell
Gp Capt Steve Townsend, Station Commander
Sqn Ldr Wes Wesley, CFS
No 45(R) Squadron:
Sqn Ldr Jad Reece, OC No 45(R) Squadron
Flt Lt Neil Cottle
Flt Lt Leon Creese
Flt Lt Leo Cheng
No 55(R) Squadron:
Sqn Ldr Andy Neal
Sqn Ldr Craig Daykin
Flt Lt Mal Prissick
Flt Lt Mal Lennon

Boscombe Down
Empire Test Pilots' School
Dave Southwood
Rhys Williams
Flt Lt Jez Robinson
Lt Cdr Jason Flintham
Lt Chris Gotke
Fg Off Leigh Hubbard
Sarah Padley

RAF Coningsby
Gp Capt Stuart Atha, Station Commander
Wg Cdr Lol Bennett, OC No 3(F) Squadron
Wg Cdr Gav Parker, OC No XI(F) Squadron
Wg Cdr Toby Craig, OC No 17(R) Squadron
Sqn Ldr Graham Pemberton
Flt Lt Andy Millikin
Flt Lt Roger Elliott
Flt Lt Antony Parkinson
Flt Lt Etienne Smith
Safety Equipment Section Nos 17(R) and 41(R) Squadrons
Groundcrews of No XI(F) Squadron
Caroline Hogg

RAF Leuchars
Wg Cdr David Hazell, OC No 56(R) Squadron
Sqn Ldr Dicko Moyes
Sqn Ldr Jonny Farrow
Flt Lt Sam Martin
Flt Lt Roddy Murray

RAF Lossiemouth
Air Commodore Mark Roberts, Station
    Commander
Wg Cdr Chris Brazier
Wg Cdr Mike Wigston, OC No 12(B) Squadron
Wg Cdr Adrian Frost, OC No 14 Squadron

Sqn Ldr Jon Greenhowe, XO No 14 Squadron
Sqn Ldr Noddy Knowles
Sqn Ldr Ian Davis
Sqn Ldr Jon Killerby
Sqn Ldr Gus McDonald
Sqn Ldr Rod Lusty, SEngO, No 14 Squadron
Flt Lt James Milmine
Flt Lt Jamie Buckle
Flt Lt Glen Allanach
Flt Lt Adam Curd
Flt Lts Ady Mellors and Rab Carruthers,
    JEngO and engineers, No 14 Squadron
Safety Equipment Section, No 14 Squadron
No 202 Squadron:
Sqn Ldr Iain MacFarlane

RAF Marham
Wg Cdr Terry Jones, OC No XIII Squadron
Wg Cdr Mike Barley, OC Ops
Sqn Ldr Dave Burrows, XO No XIII Squadron
Sqn Ldr Gordon Melville
Flt Lt Neil Taylor
Flt Lt Dave Paget
Fg Off Laurence Chapman
Fg Off Jen Shackley
Maj Marcus Prince, USAF
Capt Michiel Wintjes, RNethAF
Engineering Section, No XIII Squadron
Safety Equipment Section, No XIII Squadron

RAF Cottesmore
Wg Cdr Andy Lewis, OC No 1(F) Squadron
Cdr Kev Seymour, CO NSW
Sqn Ldr Andy McKeon
Sqn Ldr Tracey Broome
Lt Cdr Kris Ward
Maj Phil Kelly
PO Brian Beyer
AET Ash Wilkinson
AET Dan Ellerington

RAF Kinloss
Wg Cdr Iain Torrance
Sqn Ldr Mark Gunn, OC Operations
Dawn McNiven

RAF Waddington
Sqn Ldr Tim Brown
Flt Lt Cyrus Pocha
Flt Lt Simon Middleditch

RAF Brize Norton
No 99 Squadron:
MACR Spike Abbott
No 101 Squadron:
Wg Cdr Tim O'Brien, OC No 101 Squadron
Sqn Ldr Simon Blackwell
Flt Lt Ash Reed
Flt Lt Harry Stewart
Flt Lt Paul Smith
Flt Lt Nick Millikin
Flt Lt Shane Stiger
Flt Lt Graham Hannam

FS Kenny Murray
Sgt Phil Pickles
Katie Zasada
Ana Dick

RAF Shawbury
Defence Helicopter Flying School
Captain RN Martin Westwood, Commandant
Sqn Ldr John Tisbury
Flt Lt Matthew Holloway
No Sixty (R) Squadron:
Flt Lt Col Welsh
Flt Lt Si Elsey

RAF Benson
No 28(AC) Squadron:
Wg Cdr Rich Luck
Sqn Ldr Jonny Adamson
Flt Lt Matt Tandy
Sgt Steve Thomas
No 33 Squadron:
Wg Cdr Chris Luck
Sqn Ldr Chris Philpott
Flt Lt Brad Hewitt
Flt Lt Sarah Furness
Flt Lt Norm Webster
Flt Lt Rob Lakey
Flt Lt Penny Brady
MACR Kenny Laughlin
Sarah Williams
Safety Equipment Section Nos 28(AC) and
    33 Squadrons

RAF Odiham
No 27 Squadron:
Flt Lt Rich Millard-Smith
Flt Lt Andi Large
Flt Lt Mark Goodwin

The Red Arrows
Wg Cdr Jas Hawker
Wg Cdr Dave Middleton
Wg Cdr Dicky Patounas
Sqn Ldr Martin Higgins
Sqn Ldr Paula Hunt
Sqn Ldr Scott Morley
Sqn Ldr Ben Murphy
Sqn Ldr Jim Turner
Flt Lt Damo Ellacott
Flt Lt Pablo O'Grady
Flt Lt Greg Perilleux
Flt Lt Andy Robins
Flt Lt Allison Scott
Flt Lt David Slow
Flt Lt Si Stevens
Rachel Huxford
The Red Arrows Survival Equipment Section
Circus

BBMF
Sqn Ldr Al Pinner, OC BBMF
Sqn Ldr Ian Smith
Flt Lt Antony Parkinson